MW00655213

A Very Special Dedication

Having enjoyed the Ingleside Inn, I am happy that the proceeds from *Bedtime Stories of the Ingleside Inn* will benefit all of the wonderful children of the Angel View Crippled Children's Center.

With every good wish,

— Arnold Schwarzenegger

BEDTIME STORIES
OF THE
INGLESIDE INN

by Mel Haber

This book is available on cassette as read by the author.
1-800-772-6655

Lord John Press
19073 Los Alimos Street
Northridge, California 91326

ISBN: 0-935716-99-8

FOREWORD

I sort of stumbled into Palm Springs in 1975.
Somehow I wound up owning a restaurant
and hotel. My previous business experience—
which qualified me for this particular venture, was
having run an automotive accessory manufacturing
company in Coney Island, Brooklyn, for 22 years.
We manufactured hula dolls to stand in a rear
window, religious statues for the dashboard, a
tiger tail which hung out of the gas tank, etc. We
produced 750 items that did absolutely nothing!

I had the good fortune to open Melvyn's
Restaurant and the Ingleside Inn during a period
when nothing else was happening in Palm Springs.
I opened and people came because we were the new
thing in town. I made every mistake in the book but
somehow survived. In hindsight, I realize now that
had I opened in this current competitive market I
would have been bankrupt and out of business in
two months.

Many people have asked me over the years how
I came to buy the Inn, how it got started as a hotel
and restaurant, my background, etc. As I am always
looking for that extra touch to please my guests, and
the fact that I am a voracious reader, I thought having

something different to read on the nightstand of the hotel rooms was a unique idea.

Over time, I have had many experiences as the owner of an "in" place catering to the "beautiful people" and which I thought might make interesting reading. Born with the ability to laugh at myself, I dictated some of the stories, had them typed up and distributed them to a few of my regular guests. They quickly became popular and I was encouraged to offer more.

One of my regular hotel guests, Mr. Carl Bennitt, a man in the printing business, published the first edition of Bedtime Stories as a surprise gift to me. The 500 hard bound copies were sold for $25 each for the benefit of my favorite charity. Later, and by popular demand, I created Bedtime Stories II.

In the beginning of my adventure, I made attempts to find books by restaurateurs or hoteliers recollecting their experiences but, to my amazement, I found none. I found books written about them but not by them. I have had so many interesting and humorous experiences, not only in my business but in this lovely desert oasis, that any attempt to keep track of all of them would be impossible.

I have had the greatest 20 years of my life in Palm Springs and nobody is more surprised than I that I am still here and successful. Every day brings more great experiences (stories in the making) as I continue to live that fantasy of owning and operating such a place as this.

I truly hope that you enjoy reading these stories as much as I enjoyed living the experiences. So many people have been part of the Ingleside Inn's inception, progress and success and I would like to extend my personal thanks to each and every one of them for helping me to make the Ingleside Inn and Melvyn's Restaurant what they are today —
a very special place for very special people.

—Melvyn Haber

Bedtime Stories
of the
Ingleside Inn

by
Mel Haber

Lord John Press, 1988
Northridge, California

TABLE OF CONTENTS

BROOKLYN DISCOVERS
PALM SPRINGS

I t was a Saturday morning about noon, in March of 1975, and I was just hanging around my Palm Springs condominium. A fellow I knew who worked at one of the hotels in Palm Springs dropped by and suggested we take a ride. I was wearing my standard Palm Springs uniform which consisted of sneakers with no socks, cut-off dungarees, and a tee-shirt. We piled into his old convertible and started to drive through town. He talked about some property that he felt his boss should look at and asked me if I would be interested in driving through it. Having absolutely nothing else to do, I said, "Sure."

I was surprised to discover the property was virtually only two blocks from the center of town. We entered through a pair of iron gates and, lo and behold, there was this charming private estate sitting in the center of town. The entire property was secluded behind high walls. A large, circular driveway took you through it and out a gate at the other side.

The first thing you saw when you entered was a charming, Spanish-style hacienda, complete with tiled roofs and lovely vines on the wall. It was about two acres of land in a park-like setting. In addition to the main hacienda, there were several Spanish-style bungalows situated lazily around the property. There was a large veranda extending the length of the main building, and three people were seated there. It was a scene out of old-world Spain, or perhaps even Mexico.

My first impression was that the world had somehow forgotten about this property, and neglected to build the office building or stores that belong to such a great location. The property had charm and atmosphere as only a piece of property could have that had been built many years before.

As we drove through the two acres, I was really impressed with the charm and beauty of the place. It was obvious that it was suffering from neglect and needed a great deal of rejuvenation. But its intrinsic charm could not be denied. My friend asked if I would like to stop and look inside, and I said, "Sure." At this point I was thrilled just to have something to do for a couple of hours.

We took a tour of the main building. The interior looked like an old European inn and was even more charming than the exterior. First we went through the Lobby, which had a large fireplace built into the wall. There were high ceilings from which hung chandeliers, and what seemed like very valuable pieces of furniture were scattered about.

A gentleman came out from behind a registration desk and introduced himself as the manager. He said he was representing the owner who was totally inactive and anxious to sell the property. He didn't sound like a Californian and was obviously an Easterner. Upon chatting with him, I discovered he was from the "Borscht Belt." That is the Catskill Mountain region of New York State with which I was very familiar, having worked there as a teenager. It was a kind of haven for Jewish people with money. He was definitely Jewish, but this was only significant in light of the history of the Ingleside Inn. He told us that it was originally a private estate and had been turned into a hotel in 1935. He explained that from the first day and up to the present time, it was totally anti-Semitic—almost to an extreme. The present owner was from San Francisco and substantially wealthy. He had been a former guest of the woman who originally made it into a hotel. She had run it very successfully for 30 years, catering only to the blue bloods of the world, and discriminating against everyone other than pure "Wasps." Fascinated by the history he was unraveling, we sat down on the beautiful veranda, and he filled us in with more details.

He told us the Inn was originally built as a private estate in 1925 by the widow of the man who manufactured the Pierce Arrow Motorcar. It was sold in 1935 to a woman from Indiana. She ran it for the next 30 years as a very personal, private Club, and had people come primarily by invitation. She lived on the property and personally catered to their every need. She gave everyone staying at the Inn more of a feeling of being invited to someone's home rather than staying at a hotel. She was extremely successful in getting the clientele she wanted and her roster of former guests read like the *Who's Who* of the world...presidents, royalty, and captains of industry stayed at the hotel and enjoyed this lady's hospitality. The manager explained the hotel was loaded with antiques gathered by the original owner on special buying trips to Europe. He said that the value of the antiques in the hotel was probably more than the asking price of the entire piece of property.

When the woman passed away in 1965, one of her regular guests, a very substantial man from a banking family in San Francisco, bought the Inn in the hope of carrying it on in the same great tradition. However, he was totally inactive and had been absent for the greater part of the ten years he had owned it and lost a great deal of money operating it in absentia. He had presently taken sick and was most anxious to sell the property, even though he loved it dearly. The gentleman we were talking to had been hired to run the property until a buyer could be found. The manager dropped a few names of people who had stayed at the Inn such as Howard Hughes, J.C. Penney, Krupp of the German munitions family, Giannini who built and owned the Bank of America, Lily Pons who had lived there for 13 years, and on and on and on. I was absolutely fascinated by the story.

He then asked us if we would like to see the restaurant, which we didn't even know existed. He took us down to a little house at the end of the property, and when we walked in, I couldn't believe my eyes. It was about 12:30 in the afternoon, approximately 90–95 degrees outside and, as I said, my friend and I were dressed very casually in cut-off dungarees and sneakers with T-shirts. In the restaurant were twenty couples having lunch. The average age of the people sitting there would be around 70 years, I guess. The ladies were dressed "for tea" in long dresses and every man was wearing a jacket and tie.

I commented to the manager that I felt awfully warm, and he replied that there was no air conditioning. My thoughts were that this was either a sound stage setup and a movie was being shot or these people were dead and forgot to fall over. I couldn't believe my eyes! If I were going to set the stage for a meeting of the Daughters of the American Revolution or the Sons of the Original Settlers of America,

I could not have done a better job.

The restaurant was decorated in rose-colored flocked wallpaper, with burgundy drapes and burgundy carpeting. The waiters had a look about them as though they belonged there The only thing I could find missing from the whole picture was a strolling violinist. The contrast between the Jewish manager I was talking to, and the obviously Waspish clientele struck me as a pre-arranged comedy routine. He greeted a few of the people very politely in soft tones, of course, and I wasn't sure whether this thing was on the level, a comedy routine, or someone was just trying to drive me mad.

I couldn't wait to get out of there because I never felt more out of place in my life. The manager then offered to show me several of the hotel rooms. Each room was different but they all had a feeling similar to my grandmother's living room back in New York. The only way I could describe this whole experience is to say it was absolutely "trippy." I felt I had been transported back in time one hundred years.

He showed me two different basements (a rarity in Palm Springs) where I relished looking at what appeared to be valuable old pieces of furniture, newspapers, draperies, etc. Kiddingly I asked if this did not originally belong to the Collier Brothers (they were very famous wealthy recluses in New York and when they died, and their apartment was searched, it was discovered they had never thrown anything away in their entire lives). He showed us fifteen full drawers of index cards of former guests. I thumbed through some of them and actually got goose pimples. The names I ran across were legendary to me. I found a registration card on Salvador Dali, the famous artist, on which had been penciled "I believe he is a painter." There was one for Elizabeth Taylor that said "Movie Actress" and several question marks after it. There was a card for Mr. and Mrs. Samuel Goldwyn of Hollywood, California, and someone had penciled in "No Good. They're Jewish." Another card read "Earl Martyn" and penciled alongside was "Howard Hughes, wants no one to know."

At this point I must explain something about myself. Number

One, I had just sold a piece of real estate and was looking to reinvest the money in another piece of real estate. Number Two, throughout my entire life I have been presented with thousands of different business propositions. I had never heard of a business proposition that didn't sound good to me. By this time two hours had passed and I was foaming at the bit to buy this property. I was sure that after I owned it I would find the treasure of Sierra Madre buried in the ground right on the property.

It made me think of a story my father used to tell about two peddlers on the East side of New York who owned mens clothing stores. What they would do was to take a piece of paper that felt like money, fold it up and leave it in one of the pants pockets amongst the suits they were selling. When a customer would try on the suit and put his hand in the pocket, he would feel the "money" there, assume that someone who had tried on the suit had left the money by mistake. They would quickly buy the suit only to find they had been duped. I wasn't sure if I was being baited or if the whole situation was real. The asking price on the property was, I felt, very realistic—for the land value alone.

My tendency my whole life has been to act first and think later. My friend left me there and the manager and I sat down. Quickly I made an offer 25% under what he was asking (this method always made me feel I was getting a bargain, and people who know that routine simply mark up what they were trying to sell by 30%, so that one would be allowed to play my game and still win). He said my offer was ridiculous and that the property was worth every dime of the asking price. My heart was palpitating and my brain was spinning so fast I was beginning to get a headache. I suggested I come over the following morning at 10 o'clock and have coffee with him and see if we could work something out. He came up with the standard seller's comment that if I was seriously interested, I would have to move fast because there were several other people interested in the property and he would probably be selling it in a couple of days. His comment had the desired psychological effect. Immediately I experienced panic and anxiety over the possibility of losing the deal. His comment seemed to work, and by the time I left I was promising him a rather large commission if I got the property at my price. He said I was in luck since it was the weekend and nothing could transpire until we met again. I thanked my lucky stars for this piece of good fortune. I left, pacified that he would be kind enough to let me buy the place and not sell it to someone else.

I did not sleep at all that night, contemplating the many possibilities of the Ingleside Inn. With my vast knowledge of the restaurant and hotel business, which was zero, I started to scheme every angle I could as to what I would do with the property. The manager had told me that the overhead, including mortgage, utilities, the gardeners, and the chef was approximately $5,000 a month. My first thought was to find four friends and buy the property as partners. We would draw lots for blocks of four rooms each (the property had 20 rooms) and we would then each own 20% of the property. We would have our own private dining room and our own chef. It seemed a lot better than buying five separate condominiums. We would then have the right to do anything we liked with our four rooms. We could either combine them to make one luxurious suite for ourselves, or keep them as four separate rooms and have relatives and friends use them as they saw fit. That was the Number One idea. The second idea I thought of was to turn it into a health club, commonly known as a Fat Farm, for women. Two acres in a magnificent setting in the middle of Palm Springs is a natural for women to use while their husbands are playing golf. My mind was flitting feverishly. As I look back, it is interesting that at no point did I ever consider leaving it as the restaurant and hotel it was.

The following morning I drove through the property thirteen different times and each time had different ideas as to what I was going to do with it. At 10 o'clock I was waiting anxiously on the veranda for the manager to appear. He showed up at five minutes after ten, we exchanged good mornings, and went into the restaurant to have a cup of coffee. As soon as we were seated, a young man appeared at the table. He seemed to be about twenty years old, stood about 5'11," weighed approximately 150 pounds, and when he spoke to the manager, his thick, Southern drawl was, I guessed, from the Ozark area. He was wearing a shirt and tie which was certainly a rarity in Palm Springs, especially in the morning. The manager introduced him as the bellman, bookkeeper, desk clerk and assistant manager of the Ingleside Inn. The manager gave him some instructions, and he left. The manager then explained that the young man was his assistant. He paid him $300 a month, plus room and board. The young fellow worked approximately twenty hours a day, seven days a week, performing all the various functions.

We continued discussing the Inn when I noticed a middle-aged woman picking flowers in the garden of the restaurant. The manager informed me she was the housekeeper, maid and secretary. He said that between the young boy and the woman, the three of them ran the entire property. He pointed out that the restaurant had its own staff consisting of a chef, who had been working on the property for twenty years, one woman who helped him, and four odd little waiters who would have looked right at home in an English drawing room.

The hotel had always been on what is commonly known as the American plan, which means that hotel guests receive three meals a day included in the price of the room. The dining room was closed to the public and it was considered quite an honor for an outside guest to be invited to dine there. There was no liquor license, so the guests would bring their own bottle with their name taped on it and that was their private stock for their stay. This arrangement made the people staying at the Inn feel that they were guests in someone's home.

The woman who had owned the place presided over the meals as hostess. She had named the restaurant after the chef. As the manager gave me some of the colorful background of the Inn, it became obvious that anything of consequence took place between 1935 and 1965, the period this woman owned it. He alluded to the great, interesting history of the Inn and its former guests. We spent an hour structuring various offers for the owner. I used every bit of persuasion I could summon up to convince him to make sure I got the place, and finally the key to the deal was simply to promise him he could stay on as manager and live there. With that extra bonus, he assured me he would drive to Rancho Santa Fe where the owner lived and personally appeal to him on my behalf.

He called the owner and made an appointment to see him that evening with the offer. I assured him I would stay over in town until Monday so we could open escrow if my offer were to be accepted. That evening about 10 o'clock, I got the call that I had the deal. Then I proceeded to get butterflies in my stomach and a nervous headache. I slept restlessly that night and Monday morning I opened escrow to buy the Ingleside Inn.

Looking back in retrospect, I could have no idea as to how that day would affect the rest of my life.

Now what?

I now owned the Inn and a restaurant called "Orville's," named after the chef who had been there so long. I had inherited along with the hotel, a staff consisting of a funny looking 45-year-old fat man with a limp, a toupee and a very Jewish demeanor, who was my manager; a 20 year-old boy from Arkansas with an incredible drawl who was my Bell Captain, bellman, bookkeeper, and front desk clerk; a chef who was temperamental, totally absorbed with pornography, and who had never cooked for more than 50 people at a time; a lovely housekeeper who picked fresh flowers for the rooms, but who had a bad back and had difficulty making beds; and four little 60-year-old waiters, one of whom was an Englishman who called everyone 'Mum' and 'Dad,' with the net result that most customers were offended.

In the short period of a week, between the time I found the Ingleside Inn and closed the deal, I had approached the only three people I knew in California to go partners with me. Their response was unanimously 'no' for varying reasons. One sent an expert friend of his to look at the property and evaluate it. He concluded it had no chance because it only had 20 rooms. Another friend from Los Angeles drove down and told me I was crazy. "What do you see in the property anyway?" he asked. Another friend had no money. I couldn't help but feel they thought I was nuts. Nevertheless, I went straight ahead. One of the guys who turned me down was, at this point, my closest friend. His name was Bobby and he had a house in Palm Springs where I spent every weekend before I bought my condominium. By a simple process of elimination, and perhaps because I knew no one else in Palm Springs, he became my confidante and advisor.

Now I started to deal with the realities of my folly. My first concern was to find someone who could manage the property and at least maintain the small amount of income it was generating. I was content to leave the manager I had inherited there, but I wanted someone, in addition, to be my representative on a daily basis as business commitments in Los Angeles precluded my spending a great deal of time in Palm Springs.

Bobby and I were having coffee in his house one morning, when he suggested a certain local Baptist minister as the ideal manager. It seemed with that background I would at least get an "honest shake." Although I had made a deal with Morris, the manager, who came with the property, I felt I needed my own man in there. I would leave Morris with the responsibility of running it on a day-to-day basis, but I wanted someone else there full-time to represent me.

A meeting was set up and based on my history of hiring everyone I ever have interviewed, I made a deal with my new General Manager, Luther, the Baptist minister. He had a background as a general contractor and he would be in charge of construction, decorating, controlling the money, and relieving Morris when necessary. The contrast between the tall, lean, slow-talking (with a drawl no less) Baptist minister, and the short, fat Jewish guy with a limp and toupee, was something to behold.

My entire staff was now rounded out. The only problem was that this crew of misfits would have been more appropriate for a slapstick comedy than a hotel and restaurant. Now that I owned this hotel and restaurant in Palm Springs and had my crew selected, I had no idea what to do next. My whole life, the pattern has been the same. First I spend a great deal of time and effort digging myself into a big hole. Then I spend a great deal of time and effort digging myself out of the big hole. If successful, I would eventually wind up exactly where I started. From all reports I got, Barron Hilton was not in the least scared about my entry into the hotel industry.

Now that I was the owner, I started to formulate ideas and plans. I honestly don't remember at what point I decided to keep it as a hotel and restaurant, but I felt that with minor improvements I could keep it going the way it was, and even generate a little profit until I had more concrete ideas. Luther's (my Baptist general manager) experience as a general contractor would help to implement the work that had to be done. I didn't have a great deal of money to spend and my friend Bobby volunteered to help me decorate the property. He prided himself on being very artistic and creative.

Bobby lived with his girlfriend, Judy. She was a nice girl, quite content to spend her entire life in their Palm Springs home shuffling from the bedroom to the kitchen and back to the bedroom. If Judy never had to get dressed or go outside, that would be just fine with her. Bobby had a pattern similar to mine. He went to Los Angeles during the week for business, he was a salesman, and he returned every weekend to Judy and Palm Springs. I put Bobby in charge of decorating the property.

When he came down on Fridays, he would collect his girlfriend, come over to the hotel and start barking orders, "Judy, paint this trim, mirror the ceiling, make a built-in over this wall, get a flowered spread," etc., etc. She would sit like a secretary taking notes as he barked orders with all the authority in the world. He would spend about two or three hours doing this. He reminded me of a general issuing battle plans.

He would then march off quite content with himself. It was

almost as if all he had to do was to say it for it to be done. I would sit in awe watching his creativity flow. After these sessions were over, reality would set in, and I would start to wonder how all these directives would be accomplished…and how much they would cost. As they left, Judy would always give me that puzzled look, as if to say, "What happens now?" Whether his plans would be carried out or not, or if they were economically feasible never seemed to enter his mind. This went on every Friday and Saturday for about six weeks. On Mondays he and I would return to Los Angeles and Judy would return to her very contented life-style of doing no more than shuffling from her bedroom to the kitchen and back again. On certain days of the week she didn't even do that. She simply spent the whole day in her bedroom.

Two months passed by, and Luther started to tear apart the rooms so that Bobby's ideas could be implemented. Suddenly one day it dawned on me that not only had nothing been done but I was worse off than when I started. Six rooms which had been shabby but rentable were now torn apart. And a great deal of money had been spent. Nothing had been planned, ordered or done to get them back into shape although Judy did have about 50 pages of notes.

During the same period of time, I was very busy in Los Angeles formulating plans and ideas. I was working on brochures, a logo, stationery, where to buy toilet paper and towels wholesale, merchandising ideas, etc. My consultant-advisor-friend Bobby had put me in touch with a well-known public relations firm in Beverly Hills which had a clientele that could run the Academy Awards ceremony without any outsiders.

The public relations firm condescended to accept me as a client because I was a friend of Bobby's. This was my first contact with a PR firm and, based on their fee, I knew my hotel would be as famous as the Waldorf-Astoria in a short period of time. I met with them at least twice a week and discussed the various items I would need. I was primarily looking for a color scheme, and a "look" for stationery, napkins, matches, etc., as a theme of identification with the public.

My one and only contribution to the physical improvement of the Ingleside Inn was the idea that it was absolutely essential to add a jacuzzi to the property. My manager assured me that he could do it that without any problem.

As the weeks passed, more and more of my time and brain power was devoted to this project. The pervading feeling was that things were happening. Bobby and Judy were decorating the place, Luther was having the jacuzzi built, and the PR firm was working on a logo and theme. I was personally very busy writing orders for toilet paper and soap.

Over the next two months I traveled to Palm Springs every Thursday evening and spent Friday and Saturday with Bobby and Luther, reviewing that week's work. All day Sunday would be spent organizing my notes and making lists to be accomplished in Los Angeles during the coming week. Mondays I would return to Los Angeles and try to conduct some of my regular business where, incidentally, I was *making a living* running an automotive novelty business. This effort was interwoven with my meetings with my PR firm and different toilet paper salesmen.

My weekend meetings in Palm Springs were always held in a corner table in the restaurant. This was primarily because in every movie I had ever seen the owner had his special table and there always appeared to be an endless flow of people to it. I enjoyed playing this role.

Two months passed by very quickly and I decided it was time to regroup. I planned a series of meetings for the coming weekend to see where everything stood. It seemed like a number of things were in process but nothing seemed to get finished. I had already gone through quite a sum of money and I was getting scared that things were out of hand.

I had paid the PR agency for two months and so far had received nothing. From Day One, I had insisted that in order to capture the charm of the place they had to personally see it, but by this point, they had not done so. The head man finally agreed to meet me in Palm Springs on Saturday. From Los Angeles I telephoned my generals and set up separate times and meetings with each one for that weekend.

Saturday morning at approximately 10 a.m., the public relations guy arrived and I promptly took him on a tour of the facilities. We spent about 45 minutes looking at everything and then sat down for a cup of coffee. He said he had put a lot of thought into making this project successful. I waited anxiously to hear the great words to come from the creative genius who was to make me successful. He spoke very slowly, for dramatic affect, and said, "Mel, we've got to keep this property clean. I noticed several things lying around I could point out to you such as cigarette butts, discarded papers, etc.!"

After regaining my composure, I assured him I was aware of the importance of what he was saying and the astuteness of his observation. I apologized and explained that we were renovating and therefore everything was in the midst of change. I was too frustrated to say anything else and simply told him I would call him during the next week. I thanked him profusely for coming down and especially for the profound piece of advice. He left with a feeling of being truly appreciated.

The next meeting on the agenda was with Morris, the Resident Manager. During the initial two-month period, the hotel and restaurant had been functioning but doing a relatively small amount of business. The best I could determine was that I had a partner of whom I was unaware. It had dawned on me that when my receipts were $700 in the restaurant somehow only $350 wound up in the bank. I did not know if I really had a right to complain because at least my unknown partner was fair enough to split it down the middle. My meeting with Morris provided no answers...only a hurt look on Morris's face. He said he couldn't explain the missing money because Luther was the general manager. There was no doubt that Morris was not a member of the Brotherhood of Christians and Jews.

So far I had accomplished nothing and could hardly wait to have my meeting with Luther. I had about half an hour to kill, so I started wandering around the property making notes. I wandered over to my pride and joy, the new jacuzzi. It was not quite finished, and to my horror, I noticed a serious crack in the bottom.

Luther and I sat down to coffee, and reviewed some of the work in progress. At my friend Bobby's direction, six rooms had been torn apart but Luther wasn't quite sure what came next. The jacuzzi was coming along nicely, and between the electric and pool work, Luther said it would probably run only about $50,000. Luther said if I didn't have his expertise, it would have cost $65,000. I couldn't believe my ears. The jacuzzi was worth, tops, $15,000 (probably a little less with a crack in the bottom).

I then questioned him about the missing revenue, and he said that probably Morris had taken it. He apologized for having to run but he had some important business to take care of at the church. I was left sitting in a coma; I felt like screaming but did not want to alarm the six customers I had in the restaurant. *What in hell had I gotten myself into?*

After staring into space for about an hour, I came to a decision. The reality that stung the hardest was the fact that I'd have to give up the regular paycheck which had been my security for 22 years. No matter what other business deals I'd been involved in that regular paycheck had always been there. Now I would have to give up my job of 22 years and move to Palm Springs in order to protect my investment. On July 4, 1975, I packed my car and moved to Palm Springs to launch a new career and a new life.

The first thing I learned about Palm Springs was that the weather was so hot in the summer that there was little in the way of business for a hotel/restaurant operation and in those days the Inn had no air-conditioning. So I closed the place down with the intention of finishing the renovations during the summer in order to open in September, in time for the season. I fired Luther, my Baptist-minister-manager knowing I could not afford an unknown partner. As I had discovered, he had been helping himself to a percentage of whatever business was coming in.

There was a carpenter working around the place who was from Mississippi, in his middle forties and, in the absence of anyone else, I hired him to be the foreman for the renovation work. Also, I engaged the services of two young lady decorators from Los Angeles, a decision based on their reasonable fee rather than any proven ability at their profession.

Soon I was totally absorbed in the project and came to realize that there was an incredible amount of work to be done before opening day. The major projects included: redecorating the dining room, remodeling the kitchen, building a bar and lounge area, renovating all the rooms and restoring the exterior and grounds to a presentable condition.

As I rushed about each day making lists and formulating ideas, the immensity of the project grew in my mind. I had to come up with a marketing program, create a color scheme, create a logo, order endless amounts of printing required by a hotel and restaurant such as menus, postcards, letterheads, brochures, matches, napkins, and so on, as well as making sure all the furniture, drapes, restaurant utensils and the like were taken care of. Finally, Mel Haber had found a project, a single pursuit, that could consume all his energy and time, not to mention money, which was being spent at an incredible rate.

In quick order, I began acquiring staff to work on the project. A friend introduced me to a young chef who was then living at the beach with his wife and baby. Charlie was about twenty-eight, had a jovial expression and a walrus moustache, all of which gave him the general air of what most people would call a "beach bum." He was completely dedicated to the art of preparing fine foods. I hired Charlie, and he offered the services of two friends of his from the beach to help him renovate the kitchen. I took up his offer.

Next, a nineteen-year-old guy walked in looking for work. He said he was capable of carpentry, painting and some electrical work. I hired him, and he became a sort of administrative aide to me. A friend in Los Angeles sent me two young guys named Larry and Skip who were willing to work as laborers for the summer in return for good sleeping quarters and minimum wages.

Skip was 30, very skinny and balding, and a typical intellectual type. He was attempting manual labor as one of life's great experiences. Skip and Larry were as close as peas in a pod but I was never able to figure out the attraction. Between them they had the I.Q. of about 60, but they were nice, lovable, fumbling idiots.

Whenever they painted a room, they painted themselves in a corner and couldn't get out. It was impossible to explain to them to start at the back of the room and paint their way to the door. For some reason known only to them, they found it easier to start from the moment they walked in, at the threshold of the door, and paint their way into the room. On the occasions that they went to eat, they would simply walk across the freshly painted floor and across the property to Palm Canyon Drive, to a restaurant to get some food. You never had to wonder where either of them were because the paint on the bottom of their feet would leave a nice, neat trail to follow no matter where they went. If you wanted to find Larry and Skip, you simply went to the lawn area seeking the freshest tracks leading away from the hotel or back towards the hotel. All of the rooms were being painted white so that at the end of four weeks probably the only spot on Skip that wasn't white were his privates. He managed to paint himself from head to toe as well as the rooms. I often wondered if his buddy, Larry, didn't use him as a paint roller.

Paul, the architect, had his own thing going. He was obsessed with building tables for the restaurant that consisted of cutting thousands of slats of wood and nailing them together so that you had a table top that consisted of thousands of little pieces of wood nailed together. He was very busy on that project of sawing his wood, nailing it together, and could always be found in a certain spot at any given moment doing just that. I once figured out that if he worked efficiently and diligently for one week, he could finish one table top. The fact that these tables would ultimately be covered by tablecloths and would not be seen by anybody did not deter him one bit.

The summer of 1975 had no days and no nights. It was one long blur where all I could see was work that never ended. The norm was that every project had to be redone three or four times. A combination of urgency and inefficiency resulted in everything costing twice as much as it should have.

My foreman (the carpenter) set up a command post on the floor of the dining room where he sat next to a telephone and ordered anything the various workers told him they needed. Charlie and his friends from the beach spent all their time ripping out the equipment in the kitchen. It wasn't necessary, but they had the idea that renovation meant pulling things apart so they could be put together again. They were beach types who persisted in going barefoot, consequently, they spent a good part of the day removing splinters from their feet.

Jay, the young guy who became my assistant, worked around the clock with me every day, and I came to really respect him. No matter what I needed he would always come up with something. When I arrived at work at three o'clock in the morning, I'd find him asleep on the diving board near the pool. He said it was cooler sleeping outside. His big hassle in life was dealing with Larry and Skip who spent most of their time hiding rather than painting and were generally useless.

One particular incident sticks out as typical of the entire project. I had arrived at the hotel at approximately 3 a.m. to get my head together and make lists and schedules for the day. That week the emphasis was on building the bar in Melvyn's. I went down to the restaurant area to inspect the progress of the bar itself. I was seated at the bar and, for some reason, I was not able to face where the bartender would be standing. I had never been a great one for bars but I knew that whenever I had sat at a bar I had been facing the bartender. I was really confused and sat racking my brains as to what was wrong...my stool was right next to the bar and I could only sit sideways and not face the bartender. It took me an hour and a half to discover that we had forgotten to put the ledge on the bar. The consequence was that if you sat facing the bar, you had no room to put your legs in front of you. Rather than being discouraged that someone had forgotten the overhanging ledge, I was excited at finding the solution to the problem in only two hours.

Theoretically, Charlie, the chef, was in charge of the entire restaurant, and when I confronted him about the bar that morning, he had no time to deal with the problem as he was busy moving kitchen equipment around for the third time. I was to discover later that Charlie tore the kitchen apart three times and when he put it back together, he forgot to put in a pantry area which is an essential element in a commercial kitchen and without which you cannot function.

As the month of August started to disappear on us, I had a big pep rally to explain that we had to work harder as Labor Day was quickly approaching. For some reason I had fixed in my mind that Labor Day signaled the beginning of the season, and I was rushing at a frantic pace to be ready, although nobody ever told me that few people come to Palm Springs in September, and the menswear convention which had been coming to town in September for the past twenty years had canceled for the first time in history.

The net result was that I spent a lot of extra money and energy and effort to be ready for September, when nobody would be in town. I had a meeting with the entire crew to rally their last dying effort to get the Ingleside Inn and Melvyn's Restaurant ready.

As I looked at the entire crew assembled, all of whom I loved dearly by this time, I vowed that some day this story would be written. There was not one competent among the group! It was a sight to behold — seeing them assembled all at one time. Charlie the chef was busy picking his toenails; Paul, the architect, looked like he was anxious to get back to nailing his little tabletops; and Skip was almost invisible (seated in the back of the room in front of a white wall, and being painted white from head to toe, he just blended into the wall). Anyway, they all swore their undying dedication and fullest energies to finishing the job in the next few weeks.

Trucks and shipments started to arrive from the decorators, and certain finishing touches were finally being put in place. I cannot describe the elation I felt to see certain things coming to life after all that work.

Over the summer, many locals had stopped by the Inn to see what was happening. The word was all over town that some "slick guy from New York" with plenty of money had taken it over.

I received a lot of advice, opinions and comments. Most of the people knew the Ingleside Inn during its heyday, and were personally acquainted with the prior owner, Ruth Hardy. I had heard many fascinating anecdotes and stories about its history. On many occasions rummaging through the various storage areas on the property, including two basements, I came across interesting old articles, records, documents and so forth, and I promised myself that one day I would go through them thoroughly.

I was able to piece together that many years ago Ruth Hardy had come to Palm Springs from Indiana. She had taken over another small property, ran it for a year or two, and then bought the Ingleside Inn in 1935. From 1935 to 1965, Ruth Hardy somehow managed to establish the Inn as the only place in Palm Springs for the most important people. The Inn operated six months of the year and closed the other six months. She lived on the property and ran the Inn as if the people were house guests, catering to their every whim and desire. With only twenty rooms and a dining room exclusively for hotel guests, she was able to give a very personal feeling to everyone. Guests were carefully screened for breeding, background and manners, and if they were the slightest bit out of line according to her standards, they were not allowed back. She catered to royalty, presidents — the top echelon in the arts and professional worlds. Ultimately, Ruth Hardy went on to the City Council in Palm Springs and was responsible for lighting the palm trees on the main street, Palm Canyon Drive. She passed away in 1965 and the town appropriately honored her memory by naming a Ruth Hardy Park.

The second week in September, the Society Editor of the only

21

newspaper in Palm Springs called to tell me she wanted to do a historical focussed article on the Ingleside. It seems that once a year the paper did a progress edition, describing the history and progress of the various towns that comprised the desert community. I was pretty excited, and we made an appointment to meet. The editor showed up on a typically busy day when my main concern was riding herd on my crew. I had told her on the phone that I had discovered a basement crammed with old papers. I knew this article was going to be important to me but I had no idea how to sift through these documents.

As we were discussing the problem, a tiny lady of about fifty interrupted us to say she would like to speak with me. Over the course of the summer, I was constantly being interrupted by people wanting to sell me something such as advertising or services. I explained to the lady that I would be tied up for a while but she insisted on waiting. I returned to the editor and apologized that I was unable to work with her personally but would assign someone to help her. I took her into the filthy, cluttered basement and left her with one of the boys to assist her in going through the papers.

After totally forgetting about the little lady waiting for me in the Lobby, she finally managed to corner me and said, "Mr. Haber, I know you're busy, but I just wanted to introduce myself. My name is Billy Hopkins, and I am Ruth Hardy's niece. I worked on this property for twenty years as her assistant and if you would ever like to know anything about its history, I would be happy to help you." I could hardly believe it, and asked her to repeat herself. Then I literally picked her up and physically carried her to the basement and hollered out, "Look what God sent us!" The editor was as thrilled as I was, especially since she would not have to search through the basements for the information she wanted.

This incident was to be typical of the type of good luck and fate I would experience at the Ingleside Inn over the next few years and even to the present day when my particular 'guardian angel' seems to be as interested as ever in my dreams and aspirations.

SIR JOHN

I had heard about this very wealthy titled Englishman who had just checked into a local Palm Springs hotel. Somebody mentioned he was unhappy there and was considering checking into the Ingleside Inn. He owned two rare old Rolls Royces that he had brought with him and I was told that he was quite a colorful person.

It was about 10 o'clock in the morning when two gentlemen entered the lobby. One was about 6'1", 200 pounds, a head of beautiful white hair and appeared to be about 65 years old. Accompanying him was a short stocky bald-headed man approximately the same age. The shorter man immediately reminded me of a Nazi general (my only exposure to Nazi generals was those I had seen in World War II movies, however this one was missing the monocle). They were both very well dressed. The larger of the two approached the desk, announced loudly in a very British accent, "My name is *Suh* John and I wish to see the *ownuh!*"

Overhearing this in my office I approached the two with outstretched hand and introduced myself. The taller man announced again that he was *Suh* John and introduced the other gentleman as Colonel Russell Hopf. Sir John said that he wished my very best *villuh* for approximately one year! He explained that he was presently at another hotel and was leaving because they had the audacity to charge him for a plate of cheese and crackers. He felt this should have been complimentary in view of the money he was spending there. I quickly summoned all my charm and manners in order to handle my first experience with "real nobility!"

I showed the two men the best villa in the hotel. Sir John said it would be fine with certain minor improvements. Having just opened the hotel two weeks before, I had never rented this $160.00-a-day villa. Sir John whipped out 20 crisp $100 bills and said to please credit his account with $2,000. He then inquired if we could properly care for his two Rolls Royces, feed his *drivvah* and cater to the little demands made by royalty. After assuring him that the entire staff was at his disposal, we returned to the registration desk. He signed in as

Sir John Beech, London, England, and informed me he had been personally knighted by Queen Elizabeth. He casually mentioned he would be traveling a bit and when his room was vacant we should keep tabs on it for him. He said he would be more than happy to pay for the room although he would not be there much of the time. Just at that moment the Bell Captain elected to inform me that the hotel limousine had broken down. Upon hearing this, Sir John announced, "As long as I will be staying here, feel free to use my Rolls Royces for the convenience of your guests." That magnanimous offer floored me and I remember thanking my lucky stars for sending Sir John to me. After seeing to it that Sir John was moved from his former hotel and had settled in comfortably, I immediately called the entire staff from both the restaurant and hotel together. I informed them that we had visiting royalty and that he was to be accorded every courtesy and convenience humanly possible. This business was going to be even more fun than I had anticipated!

I arrived at the restaurant at my usual 7:30 p.m. and quickly looked around the dining room for familiar faces. I had two problems when I walked around the restaurant: Number One, I had no idea what to look for so I forced my eyes to dart everywhere (at least my guests wouldn't know that I didn't know what I was doing); and Number Two, being new in town, I knew very few people and felt pretty silly, but in all the movies I have seen good restaurateurs walked around all-knowingly—so I felt I might as well play the role.

I quickly noticed Sir John wearing a white dinner jacket with a black velvet bow tie. With him was Colonel Russ Hopf and a woman that I judged to be about 55 years old. I must say that Sir John was a striking man because of his size and that head of white hair. Add to that a loud and distinct British accent, put him in a white dinner jacket in an elegant dining room, and you really have a dramatic effect, to say the least. Central casting in Hollywood could not have done better.

As I approached the table to say hello, I immediately noticed a bottle of Dom Perignon (but of course!). I was introduced to Irene, Sir John's secretary of 20 years and he invited me to have a glass of champagne with them. Sir John was talking about his experiences during World War II where he played an important part in the CIA and had been consequently decorated. I sat through the entire meal with them, fascinated by the stories of intrigue during the war. Everybody in the restaurant noticed Sir John because he spoke with such a loud and distinctive voice. After dinner I joined them in the back of the Lounge for an after-dinner drink. I was fascinated when Sir John spoke about his Arabian horses, his turquoise mines in Arizona, his current acrimonious divorce, and his desire to get away from it all in the desert. I went home that night feeling honored to have the likes of Sir John staying in my hotel.

The next three days passed uneventfully with my illustrious guest. He took all of his meals in the restaurant and always made his presence known. He was constantly accompanied by his secretary and the Colonel. The third night he was there we were having a drink at the bar when Frank Sinatra walked in. Immediately Sir John went up to him, shook his hand and reminded Mr. Sinatra that they had met at one of Frank's Command Performances for the Queen of England. Mr. Sinatra acknowledged the comment, was very courteous, and proceeded with his party to the Lounge area. Sir John then recounted all the brilliant details of that night, emphasizing the fact that whenever he was in England, the Queen always invited him to all the Command Performances.

In the few days that Sir John had been at the Ingleside Inn, he managed to make sure that everyone, both employees and customers, were aware of his story. He talked about his illustrious career with the CIA, being knighted by the Queen of England, his turquoise mines, his stables of Arabian horses and the very unpleasant divorce he was in the midst of. Several times a day people would call me aside and ask me, "Is Sir John for real?"

I satisfied all questions by pointing to his two Rolls Royce cars and mentioning he had paid me in advance, in addition to the fact that Colonel Hopf's constant company seemed to verify his credibility.

During the first ten days, Sir John firmly established himself as visiting royalty and the word quickly spread that the Ingleside Inn was the place for royalty. As he became more at home, the more of a character he became. He requested 100 sets of hotel stationery so that he could inform all of his royal and celebrity friends that the Ingleside Inn was the only place for them. Sensing I was new to the business with no following, he at once took a personal interest and assured me that he would help to make the Ingleside Inn into what I dreamed it to be. Nobody could have been a better goodwill ambassador. Wherever he went, to shops, parties, etc., he would announce he was permanently residing at the Ingleside Inn. Sir John, being the dashing and flamboyant character he was, completely took Palm Springs by storm and was invited to almost all of the social events.

Arriving one morning at 6 a.m., I found Sir John swimming in the hotel pool and he informed me that by swimming every day he was able to maintain a body that belied his 72 years. That morning I found a note on my desk to call Colonel Hopf. He answered the ringing phone immediately, and in a rather apprehensive tone, asked if I might be able to take a few minutes out of my busy schedule to have coffee with him. After assuring him that I was never too busy for him (any friend of a $160-a-day long-staying guest was a friend of mine), we made a date for 10 o'clock, and at his insistence, at a coffee shop outside the Ingleside Inn.

Needless to say, my curiosity was really piqued. At approximately 10 o'clock, Colonel Hopf came striding into Sandy's Coffee Shop in full military stride. After exchanging pleasantries, the Colonel bluntly said, and I quote, "Mel, do you think Sir John is for real?" His question did not fully register immediately. Automatically, I reviewed in my mind my impressions and doubts about Sir John, and the fact that all my doubts were allayed because of the constant company of Colonel Hopf, whom I knew from people around town to be real. The entire premise of Sir John's credibility had been shaken. It took about two minutes to regain my composure and I brilliantly said, "That's a very strange question coming from you, Colonel." He answered, "Mel, if I wasn't at the point of total frustration, I wouldn't be here right now." He went on to say, "Let me tell you what I know about Sir John. About three weeks ago, somebody told me this titled Englishman had arrived and was looking to purchase some Rolls Royces. Well, I had these two cars for sale and I phoned him at once and set up an appointment. I went over to meet Sir John and he was living in a magnificent suite. He came outside, looked at the cars, asked me how much I wanted for them, drove each one around the block and then agreed to purchase both of them. He asked me if I would be kind enough to loan him the cars to use until he received the funds from overseas, explaining that the reason he was buying them was to have cars in America to use. Naturally, for an $80,000 deal, I agreed. Each day he gave me another reason as to why the check had not arrived. He explained that he was involved in this divorce proceeding, and that his financial matters were a little bit complicated at the moment. The deal was big enough so that I started to spend all my time with Sir John. As I mentioned, every day he told me a different story, and the most recent one he's given me is that he is waiting for a key to arrive in the mail for a safety deposit box in Mexico. He said that as soon as he gets that key, he and I would drive down to Mexico and pick up the money for the cars. He certainly seems real enough, but I thought perhaps the fact that he has been here for ten days, you might have learned something. Since he has had the cars he has told everybody that they are his, and that he owns them. I am beginning to wonder if he did not use the cars and me to establish himself. In fact, I am beginning to have some doubts about the whole situation."

I now found Sir John even more interesting than before and assured the Colonel that on the basis of his information, I would look at Sir John with a different perspective and see if I could find out anything that would be of value to the Colonel. I returned to the

Ingleside Inn and discussed this situation with my General Manager.
It was his point of view that due to the fact that Sir John had given his
money up front, our exposure was limited, and that we would just have
to keep tabs on him.

Another ten days passed and Sir John owed me approximately
$2,500, which we requested and he promptly paid. He informed us
that he would be out of town for a few days and to make sure his villa
was kept intact. During the several days that Sir John was out of town,
many people in the restaurant mentioned that they would love to
meet Sir John, if the opportunity presented itself. I assured them that
he was around constantly when he was in town, and that there would
be no problem.

After approximately 10 days Sir John reappeared on the scene
with a very polite young man and a brand new Mercedes 450 SL. Sir
John introduced the young man as his *drivahh!* He wanted to know if
his driver would be able to take his meals with my staff. I assured him
he would be treated as one of our own. Sir John suggested that we have
a cup of coffee together so he could fill me in on the details of his
exciting trip.

We were seated in the corner of the dining room and he
proceeded to tell me that the main purpose of his trip out of town was
to receive an award for his Arabian horses, and that I should come to
his villa and see the beautiful crown they had bestowed on him as the
owner of such magnificent animals. Sir John explained that he was
finally making progress on his messy divorce and that his turquoise
mines were producing more than ever.

He told me that in the short period of time he had been staying at
the Ingleside Inn, it was like home to him and it was a great feeling to
be back. He also mentioned that the following day he was going to
purchase a large aquarium for the living room of his villa, and he felt
that the little pond in our courtyard would look lovely with some exotic
fish and insisted on gifting me with them. He said he was going in to
rest for a while but would see me at dinner and would my lady be free to

join us. After checking with her, I told him it would be her pleasure.

About 6 o'clock that evening, Sir John entered the Lounge, beautifully attired in an elegant white dinner jacket with a black velvet bow tie, making his usual striking appearance. He was carrying several gift-wrapped boxes. He gave one to my manager, one to my son, and one to me, saying that he had found a great men's shop in town that afternoon. He had loved the merchandise and had gone on a spending spree. It seems he had purchased about $3,000 worth of clothing on his good name. He fell in love with a certain shirt and felt the important people at the Ingleside Inn should have them as his gift. When my lady appeared, he presented her with a gold goblet, and with all the appropriate pomp and ceremony, proclaimed he was "dubbing" her "Lady Carol" and that never again would she drink out of an ordinary glass but only out of this special gold goblet. At this point he really must have had a hell of a trip as his benevolence was overflowing. "Lady Carol" and Sir John dined together, and I must tell you, they made a striking couple.

After dinner we all went back to the Lounge to listen to our regular singer, and have our after dinner aperitif. Sir John was seated in his regular seat which had become known as the Throne, and people quickly gathered around him. As fate would have it, there was a socially prominent couple from Newport Beach in the audience and they were absolutely thrilled over the experience of meeting Sir John. By the end of the evening they were all the best of buddies and promptly invited Lady Carol, Sir John, my singer and myself, to their daughter's wedding which was to take place in two weeks. They would send a private jet to pick us up for the wedding, and assured us that it would be the social event of the year in Newport Beach. One thing was obvious. It did not take Sir John long to charm anyone he wanted to. The entire evening was fascinating to behold as people presented themselves to Sir John as if he were the Pope, and the only thing missing was the ritual of kissing the ring on the Pope's finger.

The following morning the thing that I remember most was the flow of drinks the night before. Feeling slightly hung over, I showered and shaved quickly. I was running late and it was past my normal 7:00 a.m. arrival at the Inn. As I drove through the gates, I caught a glimpse of Sir John in his bathing suit, jogging back to his villa. This man would never cease to amaze me. How at 72 he could stay up that late, drink copiously and still get up at 6 o'clock in the morning to exercise was beyond me.

It was about 10 o'clock when I was summoned to the courtyard area of the hotel to witness the local pet store stocking my pond with the most magnificent fish I have ever seen. Sir John was right there supervising to make sure that everything was perfect. It was the most breathtaking array of exotic fish I have ever seen in one place before. I did not know what to say, I was speechless. I was so full of gratitude I wanted to kiss him. We then went to his villa to supervise the installation of the one-hundred-gallon aquarium he had purchased for his living room. He invited me down to take a look at it, which I did out of curiosity more than anything else.

As I approached the villa, I was stunned to see seven different bird cages hanging in the front patio with various types of birds. As I walked inside, I was overwhelmed at how beautiful the aquarium looked in the living room. I had not been in Sir John's villa since he began to occupy it, and he had really changed it around to suit his taste—right down to the fact he had a large chair, which I had never seen before, in the middle of the living room and low chairs around it as if he were holding court. What really surprised me was, as I looked around the room, I noticed many pieces of antique furniture and artifacts that had been missing from various other places in the hotel. I had been quite upset about the pieces disappearances but did not have the nerve to ask Sir John how he had obtained these articles, as I figured that the blessings of Sir John's presence far outweighed such trivia.

He then took me into the bedroom and showed me a magnificent crown on a red velvet pillow—supposedly the award for his Arabian horses. Scattered carelessly over the dresser, I noticed many large pieces of turquoise jewelry. I knew nothing about jewelry and especially turquoise but was always impressed by the many different and magnificent pieces that Sir John wore daily. I never saw the same piece twice. Sir John then excused himself as he pointed out he had a luncheon date with someone in the restaurant and had to get ready.

At about one o'clock, as I was strolling around the dining room, I noticed Sir John sitting with a woman whom I judged to be between 35-40. Sir John beckoned me over. He introduced me to Miss Jorgensen. She had a very deep, resonant voice which was out of character with her looks. Sir John was quick to point out that this was the Christine Jorgensen who had received the wide publicity as the first human being to have a sex-change operation. Sir John never ceased to amaze me.

That evening in the Lounge at about 9:30 the door opened and there was Sir John in a red velvet robe and a crown on his head. I couldn't believe my eyes!! Everyone in the Lounge turned around and stared, and then broke out in a loud, cheering applause. Sir John explained that every once in a while he enjoyed wearing his robe and crown because it reminded him of the knighthood he had received from the Queen. It didn't really matter whether this man was genuine or not, he certainly was the most colorful and flamboyant character I had ever met or even heard of.

The following day word had spread around Palm Springs about Sir John, the robe and crown, and there were even more people visiting the Ingleside Inn in the hope of getting a glimpse of Sir John. It was about two days after that incident that we could not find our gardener. Now the gardener was thirty-two years old, a skinny man, weighing approximately 130 pounds, with long, hippy-type hair, a beard, and needless to say, absolutely filthy looking. We had called his home for several hours, no answer. It was unlike him not to appear punctually every morning. Everyone was wondering where he was, when our Head Housekeeper reported that if we were looking for Roger, the gardener, he was asleep in Sir John's villa in his bed.

Alarmed that Roger might scare off the best guest I would ever have, I ran down immediately to Sir John's villa only to find Sir John sitting on his front porch having a cup of tea and playing with his birds. I started to apologize profusely about the gardener, when Sir John told me that Roger was there by his invitation as he appeared to be tired. Roger had been out the night before, and Sir John told him it was quite alright to take a nap in his bed.

Over the next few weeks at various times we found our dish-washer, bellmen, gardener and everyone else either sleeping, hanging around, "or smoking grass" in Sir John's villa. I really wasn't quite sure how to approach the situation as they were there by the invitation of Sir John himself. When I admonished one of the staff for visiting Sir John's villa, Sir John promptly called me on the carpet and said he had a right to invite whomever he wanted to his villa since he was paying for it. At this point, I was not about to upset the apple cart and was willing to concede anything to Sir John.

The next day was the day of the wedding in Newport and my schedule was too hectic to permit me to go. The private plane had arrived at Palm Springs Airport to pick up Sir John, my singer and "Lady Carol." They were a good-looking trio as they boarded the private jet for the big event. They returned that evening at about 11 o'clock with glowing reports of the lovely and impressive people that had attended the affair and how well they had been treated. To deviate for a moment, all the pictures I eventually saw of the wedding, of which there were many, very few showed the bride and groom, but rather the newspapers emphasized the fact that visiting royalty had attended, mainly Sir John, Lady Carol, and singer George Allardice from Palm Springs.

During the course of the next few weeks, the season opened up in Palm Springs and Sir John was the most sought-after guest in the city. As a general rule, I don't attend many parties, but the few I did attend, Sir John was there in all his glory, and always the center of a crowd of people. His pronouncement that he was a permanent resident of the Ingleside Inn was a two-way street, as it added prestige to the Inn and at the same time gave Sir John credibility. Anyone who could afford to stay in a $160-a-day villa on an indefinite basis certainly had to be substantial.

Two months passed with Sir John rather prominent on the local hotel and restaurant scene. By this time he knew almost everyone in town. Poor Colonel Russ Hopf was still chasing him to close the deal on the two Rolls Royces. But every day Sir John managed to string him out a little longer. His secretary was with him constantly, and his chauffeur spent every day washing the two cars, being Sir John's valet, and generally making himself available to anyone who needed help. It was not unusual for Sir John to loan out one of Colonel Hopf's Rolls Royces, along with his chauffeur—he quickly became the best-liked person in town.

In order to keep himself occupied, he had announced that he was entertaining the idea of purchasing a million-dollar home, consequently every real estate broker in town was romancing Sir John. Many of his days were spent in the back of a real estate limousine, being chauffeured and personally escorted through some of the best homes in Palm Springs. To my knowledge, Sir John never had any intention of buying a home, but just thought it was an interesting way to spend his time.

Sir John mentioned one day that he would have to make a business trip to New Mexico to take care of some affairs regarding his turquoise mines. It was at that time I had some mechanics building some special dune buggies for me, and was having difficulty registering them with the Department of Motor Vehicles in California. Sir John suggested that I jot down the serial numbers of the engines and since the Governor of New Mexico was his personal friend, he would bring me back New Mexico state registrations and license plates for the cars. He said it would then be easy to transfer them to California registration. I had nothing to lose, so I jotted down three different serial numbers on a piece of scratch paper with no legal documentation whatsoever, and gave them to Sir John. He returned approximately eight days later. He brought with him three New Mexico registrations, and three sets of license plates. I couldn't believe it.

There were many nights that I wondered about Sir John and I would always come to the same conclusion. Whatever game he was playing, I didn't see any harm in it as he was not hurting anyone. I was reasonably sure that Sir John was a fake, but nonetheless, his bill was fairly current and to my knowledge he had not asked anyone for anything. The only possibilities running through my mind were perhaps he was living out a fantasy with a few dollars he had accumulated and was going to spend it all over a few months in Palm Springs playing numero uno...perhaps he was setting up a ruse to win the confidence of some wealthy people and then con them...or perhaps the game was to meet and marry, or get money from some rich lady. On occasion, he escorted some of the best ladies around town, but he did not seem to diligently pursue that path.

Another aspect of Sir John's story was that he had produced several pictures in Hollywood, and the names and facts he mentioned were always accurate to my knowledge. At one point he had stored some very valuable movie camera equipment in the hotel safe, and even though up to that point I had no reason to distrust Sir John, I was never really worried about my bill because I always had the camera equipment in my safe, as collateral, which I figured was worth a few thousand dollars.

In my previous business life, one of my investments had been a company who manufactured a unique line of belt buckles and we were in the process of liquidating that company. Sir John claimed to be able to liquidate these belt buckles at about $1.50 apiece, and I had an inventory in the basement of about 3,000 pieces. I knew that sooner or later Sir John's bubble would have to burst but I was not sure how it would come about, or what exactly would take place.

Sir John mentioned that he was planning a trip to New Mexico in about two weeks and that he would take the belt buckles with him and would sell them. In the interim, Sir John was becoming even more prominent in town and approximately two days before his scheduled trip, the local newspaper devoted the entire second page of its edition to Sir John, entitled "Royalty Invades the Desert." It was a very impressive interview.

Two days later, Sir John was planning to leave and mentioned that he had to take the camera equipment to New Mexico, he gave me some story as to why. I checked his hotel bill and found it was the largest balance since he started staying with me, approximately $4,200. He was going to take the only security I had, the $4200 hotel bill would be open, and additionally he was going to take $3,000 worth of belt buckles with him because allegedly he could sell them there. I had an ominous feeling that this was the end. The circumstances seemed right but I did not know how to confront him about it. If anything was going to happen, it would happen now. That night in the restaurant, Sir John approached me and said, "Please take care of my two Rolls Royces while I am gone." Now I was really stuck because I knew the cars were not his. This would be the first time he would be gone when I would be left with no security.

About then I received a phone call from a singer in Los Angeles whom I had met in my restaurant, and with whom I had become very friendly. She called to invite Sir John and myself to the opening of a nightclub in Los Angeles that night and said she would be most honored if both Sir John and I would attend. It was impossible for me to go as it was going to be a very busy night in the restaurant, but I conveyed the message to Sir John who was absolutely delighted and flattered and said that he could postpone his trip to New Mexico to attend the opening. He begged me to go with him, but I excused myself on the pretext of business. He then lined up two or three other people in town with whom he had become friendly, and they planned a big night in Beverly Hills for the opening.

The entourage left for Los Angeles at approximately 5 o'clock in the evening. At 6 o'clock that evening, Palm Springs Police came into the restaurant with a warrant for the arrest of Sir John. When I questioned them as to what it was about, they told me it was a bad check charge from Michigan. I explained to them that he had gone out of town and was expected to return the following morning. The word that there was a warrant out for the arrest of Sir John spread through Palm Springs like wildfire.

At approximately 8 p.m. that evening, Sir John called me from Los Angeles and said he had heard the police were looking for him and he wanted to know what it was all about. When I explained it to him, he said there must be some mistake. He asked if I could please find out more about it and he would call me back in an hour. I checked with the Palm Springs Police who advised me they were going to stake out his room and when he called back I was to keep him on the line so they could trace the call.

An hour later I received his call while in the Lounge. In the meantime, the police had taken over his villa, closed off access to anyone, and set up a system whereby they could trace his call. I immediately sent a waiter to tell them Sir John was on the phone. I stalled Sir John on the phone in the Lounge for several minutes. I explained to him that there was so much noise in the Lounge I could not hear him clearly and asked him to please hold on while I went to another area of the Lounge. Then I told him something had come up in the restaurant and asked him to please hold on another minute. Then I went to the men's room, washed my hands, dilly-dallied, and came back. He was still on the phone and I spoke to him for another five minutes—stalling for the police. He explained the bad check had to be a mistake. He kept repeating that there had to be some mistake, and that he would be back in the morning to clear up the whole matter.

I hung up the phone and ran to Sir John's villa to see if the police had tracked the phone call. They told me I had not kept him on the phone long enough. I couldn't believe it! At that moment, there was a knock on the door of the villa, I opened it and saw Tony, Sir John's driver, standing there. He told me he had come to pack Sir John's belongings for the trip to New Mexico. The police immediately brought him in and started to question him about Sir John. It didn't take Tony long to break down, He explained that approximately one week before showing up at the Ingleside Inn, he had been hitchhiking when Sir John picked him up and told him he was going to be his personal valet, that he was not to say anything but to go along with whatever he, Sir John, said and to play the role of driver/valet. Tony said he didn't know anything about Sir John other than that as a result of meeting him he was living pretty well.

Tony had been staying with Sir John's secretary and she had just received a phone call from Sir John that instructed Tony to go to his villa and collect all of his things. Tony had driven over in the secretary's car, a four-seater Mercedes. He was supposed to return to the secretary's apartment and Sir John would call him later, telling him where they would meet. The police went out and searched the secretary's car. In the trunk, they found a television set from the hotel. Tony swore he had no idea how it got there.

The police decided to keep Tony in the villa so he could have no communication with Sir John. He was to spend the night in the villa, along with a policeman, and await Sir John's arrival the next day. Sir John called me several times during the evening to try and pump me for information as to what was going on, but I did not let on anything about Tony or that the police were waiting for him. Needless to say, the next day came and went and Sir John never appeared.

There is a law to protect innkeepers, the Innkeepers Protection Law, which gives an innkeeper the right to impound any possessions of a guest until the bill is paid. The police carefully pointed out to me that everything in that villa belonged to me until I got paid.

The following day the police told me I should take everything in the villa and lock it in my safe until further developments. They went through all of Sir John's personal possessions and I do not know what they found. The following morning when I was in my office around 7 a.m., one of the bellmen ran up to me and said, "Somebody is removing something from Sir John's villa." Quickly I rushed down there and found the detective who had spent the night there, moving the aquarium. I called him over and said nothing could be removed until I was paid. The detective said he was embarrassed and wanted to talk to me privately. He said he did not know how to tell me, but he owned the pet store from where Sir John had bought the aquarium. He had extended credit to Sir John for the aquarium, in addition to the fish in my pond, but had never been paid. He was taking the aquarium back in order to recoup some of his loss. He was totally embarrassed about the whole situation. What could I say? Sir John had conned the detective along with everyone else.

While moving Sir John's belongings to my safe, we discovered 20 pairs of new shoes, maybe 50 garments, plus oodles of jewelry, as well as a couple of velvet robes and all sorts of odd things. Sir John had built up such a reputation that the people he came in contact with trusted him implicitly and had entrusted him with many valuable possessions.

The following day, Sir John called me again and tried to convince me that it was all a dastardly mistake and pleaded with me to ship his belongings to a certain address. I explained to him that I could not until I was paid, that I was sorry to have to take that position, but under the circumstances I had no choice. He tried every angle to coerce me into sending certain items to him. He said there was an attache case in which he had some very valuable jewelry plus extremely important papers, and would I please make sure to take good care of it until he straightened out this whole situation. I assured him it was in good, safe hands, and that I would take care of it pending the outcome of the whole mess.

Sir John's secretary then called me and asked if she could see me immediately, as it was urgent. I met her in the restaurant and she proceeded to tell me she had only met Sir John two months before he came to the Ingleside Inn. He had managed to persuade her that he was for real and had conned her out of $20,000 for some sort of investment. It seems for some reason she had also given him her jewelry, which was now all she had left in the world. She knew the $20,000 was gone. She asked me to please give her jewelry back to her, as now that her money was gone, she was penniless. When I asked her why she had played the role of secretary and lied for a man after he had cheated her out of her money, she explained that at that point it was just too late, the money was gone and the best she could do was to play along with Sir John hoping that, by some miracle, he could recoup some of the money and pay her back. She really had no choice, she said. I could not very well give away Sir John's belongings. However, with the police's blessing and a letter from the lady's lawyer, I allowed her to go through the several jewelry cases and pick out four pieces that belonged to her.

The next phone call I got was from a local singer in town whom I had met several times. She said she had to talk to me, and I invited her over for a cup of coffee. Her singing act was modeled after Sophie Tucker's act. She was a great fan of Sophie Tucker's and she had spent her entire life savings to buy two velvet robes of Sophie Tucker's. She used the robes in her act constantly. She had run into Sir John and he had convinced her to lend him the robes for some fun and games. She understood I had the right to keep them in my possession until I was paid, but they were hers and they represented not only a lot of money, but were of great sentimental value to her, and would I please be kind enough to give them back to her. There was no way I could deny this impassioned plea, so I dug them out of the safe and gave them to her.

At that time there was a little 70-year-old cashier working in the kitchen. She came to me with tears in her eyes and explained that she had given Sir John three diamond rings she had accumulated over the 70 years of her life. Sir John was supposed to have had them appraised and tell her what they were worth. She asked me if I had noticed them amongst Sir John's belongings. When I told her I had, she begged me to give them to her as they were all she had in the world. Needless to say, I returned the three rings to the little lady.

I started then to receive more phone calls from people all over town all concerned about money that was owed to them by Sir John. At that point I arranged with the Palm Springs Police for all the phone calls to be referred to them.

Three days passed and not a word was heard from Sir John. Early in the morning of the fourth day, I called one of the people who had gone to Beverly Hills along with Sir John to the singer's opening. As soon as the voice on the other end of the phone answered, I knew at once it was Sir John! I asked for Steve, pretending that I had not recognized Sir John's voice, but he immediately recognized mine. He immediately disguised his voice and answered that Steve was not home. I left a message to have Steve call me when he returned. At once I advised the Police Department where Sir John was located.

Two hours later the word was all over town that Sir John had a long criminal record, and according to the newspapers, he had been a house painter in Detroit. The publicity was priceless. The formal charges were Grand Larceny and Forgery in New York State, and issuing worthless checks in New Mexico. They listed eleven aliases and a record stretching from 1938 including convictions for embezzlement, unarmed robbery, and possession of an automatic weapon. According to Suffolk County Police in New York, Sir John was an East Hampton contractor and house painter and was indicted in November, 1972, after he stole a friend's car and sold it for $1,500. He forged his friend's name on the transfer. He had served time in jail on various occasions. He had been arrested a dozen or so times, beginning in 1938. He was arrested for vagrancy in Florida in 1938; embezzlement in Michigan in 1947; and, stolen property in 1951, for which he spent time in the Federal Penitentiary in Pennsylvania. He was arrested again in Michigan in 1954; in Sioux City, Iowa in 1959 for malicious attempt to extort; in New York in 1971 for a concealed weapon, where again he served time in the Federal Penitentiary.

During the arrest of Sir John, he took an overdose of tranquilizers and they had to pump his stomach. The irony of the whole story is that many local merchants visited him in the hospital, still convinced that there had been a mistake and that Sir John was really what they wanted him to be.

Two months after the incident a local attorney was hired on behalf of Sir John to pay his hotel bill and retrieve his possessions from my safe. While browsing through some of Sir John's paperwork, we found many pieces of correspondence from people with whom he had spent time in jail. We also found a check made on a Sir John Beech bank account to Universal Studios for $250,000. He had a collection of *Who's Who* books covering the movie industry, the social world, and the political world.

Sir John was a student of the wealthy and the affluent and really had studied the facts and figures to pull off the pretense that he hobnobbed and traveled with these people. He actually worked hard at his craft and he did it well.

This story is written some years after the incident and, I must tell you in all sincerity, that I and everyone else who came in contact with Sir John, only have fond memories of him. In spite of everything, all involved truly enjoyed what I am sure will be one of the most interesting experiences and unforgettable characters we shall ever meet in all of our lives.

SOME PEOPLE
HAVE ALL THE LUCK

I had just opened Melvyn's Restaurant and Lounge at the posh Ingleside Inn a week before, and was in a state of euphoria because of the many VIPs, celebrities, and notables who had walked through my doors in that short period of time. I was informed by my Maitre d' that he had just taken a reservation for the publisher of the local newspaper, Mr. Ted Grofer, who was coming with a party of four. Needless to say, I was most anxious to make a good impression with the head of the most important newspaper in Palm Springs. I told my Maitre d' that the minute his party was seated, to let me know so I could meet him.

I was sitting at the bar chatting with a customer when the Maitre d' motioned me over. He said, "I just seated the Grofer party at table 20." I pulled myself erect, straightened my jacket, checked myself in the mirror (that night I had used artificial face bronzer and I was never going to look better than this), and walked over as confidently as I could. I walked up, stretched out my hand, knocked over a bottle of wine, and said, "It's my pleasure to meet you, Mr. Grofer."

Needless to say, my facade of confidence was immediately blown. I started at once to apologize profusely and asked the guests if they would please move back from the table so I might switch the table with the one immediately next to them. The man sitting on the right of the gentleman whose hand I shook very casually said, "Number One, I am Mr. Grofer; and Number Two, don't you think it would be easier to change the tablecloth than move the table?" I giggled nervously, and explained to him that this was evidence of my long and extensive background in the restaurant business—one week.

I knew I had accomplished part of my purpose which was to make an impression. I am not quite sure that this was the impression I had wanted to create, but I had made one nevertheless. I was rescued by a message that I had a phone call. I figured that if my future in the restaurant business was going to be anything like that moment or any of the other similar experiences of the past week, my best solution was to build a series of trap doors throughout the restaurant so I could exit gracefully.

Although my primary function at night is to circulate through-out the dining room with a big smile on my face, I managed to avoid passing the Grofer table. I was absolutely new to the business and had no idea what it was I was supposed to do when I circulated. But in all the movies I had seen, a good restaurant owner always circulates with a very knowledgeable look on his face. I was grateful for the little pieces of debris and lettuce that fell on the floor during the evening as my picking them up as I walked around seemed to justify my existence.

On approximately my seventh tour of the dining room, about two hours after I had been to the Grofer table, he caught my attention and motioned me to come over to the table. He said, "Don't be embar-rassed, these kind of things happen." He said that he and his party would like to go into the Lounge and hear the entertainment for a while and asked if I would set them up with four seats. I said I would only be a minute and promptly went back and managed to secure the four best seats in the Lounge for them. I escorted his party to the back of the Lounge personally. I was feeling a lot better about the situation.

Not wanting to impose, I kept my distance for awhile and then decided to go back and see how they were enjoying everything. As fate would have it, as I was approaching the back of the Lounge, I saw the cocktail waitress slip and a bottle of wine fell over their table, soaking the entire party. Being the "stand-up guy" that I was, I immediately turned on my heels and ran out the front of the restaurant.

When I got outside, I realized I had no place to go, no place to hide, and sooner or later I would have to face the music. I sauntered back to the Grofer party and played stupid, as if I had not seen the acci-dent. When I asked how everything was going, the publisher's wife informed me about the spilled wine and that her dress was very expen-sive (her lack of understanding was only a small indicator of the height of her irritation). I offered to replace the dress—having no idea of what I might be getting into. Fortunately, she said she would settle for a good cleaning. I apologized profusely, thanked them for their under-standing, and assured them I would make it up to them.

About a week later, Mr. Grofer called me on the phone and said he wanted to entertain a group of important people and wished to make a reservation at Melvyn's. He asked if I would look after the arrangements personally. Overjoyed that I had a chance to make amends so quickly, I marked on the reservation sheet "GROFER VIP, party of six at 8:00." The reservation was scheduled for a Saturday night, which is always total chaos in Palm Springs. It is not unusual in any Palm Springs restaurant to wait a considerable time on a Saturday evening, even if you have reservations.

So many things were happening to me—I was meeting so many new people, I was new to the business and, consequently, I always felt I was in a constant state of confusion. Being one of the world's greatest list makers, things had gotten so bad that I was beginning to make notes to remind myself to take a shower and shave.

When Saturday night came, I was in an advanced state of confusion and nervous about all the reservations we had. I arrived at the restaurant at 7:45 in the evening to find a crowded foyer of people waiting to be seated. Several different people grabbed me to tell me that they knew my Aunt Tillie back in Brooklyn, or that they had gone to school with my cousin, Shelley, etc.

By the time I had worked my way to the back of the Lounge, it was 9 o'clock. Who should be sitting there but Mr. Grofer and his party. He motioned me over and very facetiously said, "We have already been waiting one hour, how much longer do you think it will be?" The tone of his voice would have kept ice cream frozen. I could not believe I had forgotten to follow up as promised. I had put it on my list but I forgot to make a note to *look* at my list. I ran back immediately to the Maitre d' and asked him what had happened. I told him that I had marked the reservation "VIP." He informed me he could not read my writing and translated the name of the party as "G. Rofen VIP."

It took about ten minutes before I was able to get Mr. Grofer and his party seated, and at this point, I figured the only article about me that would make the *Desert Sun* would be my obituary or a bankruptcy notice, depending upon which came first. My manager, who was a veteran of thirty years in the business told me not to take it so hard, but that on Monday morning I should call Mr. Grofer and invite him and his wife to have dinner at Melvyn's as my guests. Taking heart at the possibility that this might be my salvation, I couldn't wait until Monday morning to right my wrongs.

They say time is a great healer, and I sincerely believe it because when I reached Mr. Grofer Monday morning, the tone of his voice indicated that "fear is worse than fear itself." I told him that he would do me a great service if, at his convenience, he and his wife would give us another try and be my guests. He thanked me, said it was very nice of me, and that he would see if he could coerce his wife into coming back.

Now, usually I take off one weekday night in order to recoup my strength and my sanity. When I went in Friday, my Maitre d' called me over and said he had to talk with me. He said, "Mr. Haber, I don't know how to tell you this, but I goofed with Mr. Grofer last night!" I couldn't believe it and didn't want to hear the story but I had no choice. It seems I neglected to tell anybody that Mr. and Mrs. Grofer were to be my personal guests—assuming that when they wanted to come in that he would make the reservation with me personally.

According to the Maitre d', what happened was: the Grofers came in on my night off, had dinner, and as they were about to leave, he thanked the waiter and gave him a tip. He then started to walk out. The waiter, adhering to the course of his duty, said, "Excuse me, sir, but you have neglected to pay the check." I gathered, knowing the waiter, that there had been even more to it that that. Maybe he even "jumped" Mr. Grofer, as though he were trying to cheat the house! Having been confronted before several other customers, and rather embarrassed about the whole thing, it seems Mr. Grofer simply pulled out the money and paid the check. It was one of the few times in my life that I was capable of crying.

Trying to console me, my manager explained that in this business every restaurant has what they call "jinxed customers." Not knowing what else to do, I sat down and composed one of the most apologetic letters in my "oft-erring" life. I reminded Mr. Grofer that to 'forgive is divine' and that should he ever have the nerve to risk coming into my restaurant again, that I, personally, would be the doormat at the front door for him to walk on. I immediately set up a mental block about his name, and his newspaper, because the mere thought of it gave me cramps in my stomach.

Approximately a month later, on a Wednesday night, I walked into the restaurant and much to my surprise, sitting at a big center table, were six men and one of them was none other than Ted Grofer! I approached the table on tiptoes, and since at this point the whole situation was so outrageous, the first comment out of my mouth was, "I can't believe you came in here without a helmet!" Mr. Grofer replied, "Mel, I think maybe making the reservation in my name is bad luck, so we made it in someone else's name, and I thought maybe we could get away with it without incident."

He went on to say there wasn't a chance in the world that his wife would come back but that he enjoyed living dangerously. Totally relieved I went into a comic routine for his whole party explaining the "jinxed" customer routine, poking fun at myself and my lack of experience in the business, and a good time was had by all. By this time I was seated with the group and everybody was really getting off on me, primarily on my stupidity, inexperience, and all those essential qualities that make a man successful.

I must have been sitting there forty-five minutes telling my life story, of how I got into such an unlikely situation as the restaurant business and so on, when Ted Grofer suggested a toast to the new host in town. With that, he stood up to make the toast. At exactly that moment, the waiter was passing by with a tray and— need I say it—Mr. Grofer's head hit the tray and four hot entrees spilled on the table. I am not quite sure whether he was serious or kidding when he picked up a knife and made menacing gestures toward me but I didn't wait around to find out.

I simply shrugged my shoulders, walked out the front door, got into my car and went home.

I know this story sounds unbelievable, but it is absolutely true. At that stage, the whole series of episodes was so outrageous and so unbelievable that you can only laugh about it.

A few months passed and Mr. Grofer had been nowhere in sight. But, one weekday afternoon at lunchtime, lo and behold, Mr. Grofer was sitting at a table with another gentleman. There was no way I was going to go anywhere near that table. As fate would have it, it was pouring rain (unusual for Palm Springs). I was hiding in the back of the restaurant when my manager came back and said to me, "You will not believe what has just happened!"

It seems Mr. Grofer received an important phone call from his wife while he was having lunch. She told him that her car would not start and she had been on the way to pick up their son at school. She asked him to drive over and pick up the child. With that, he went outside to get into his car and discovered that after the parking lot attendant had opened the door for him to get out, he had inadvertently hit the automatic lock control for the doors and Mr. Grofer's car had been sitting there in the teeming rain, engine running, with all the doors locked. No, there's more…at the moment Mr. Grofer went outside to get into the car, it ran out of gas!

As if that were not bad enough, his car had been blocking the entrance to the restaurant so the attendants have been driving other customers' cars over my beautiful lawn in order to get the people out of the rain. I offered to drive him to pick up his son but he very wisely said, "No thank you." Not to be discouraged by his refusal of my help, I insisted he take one of my many cars. He accepted my offer, thanked me, and left.

Fifteen minutes later, my secretary informed me that a Mr. Grofer was on the phone. Pleased that he had the courtesy to call and thank me, I picked up the phone and said, "Hello Ted." In a voice that wreaked of murder, he slowly and carefully explained exactly where he was — with a flat tire!

Over time I have run into Mr. and Mrs. Ted Grofer at many social events, and we have been able to joke about it since they were no longer coming into the restaurant, and therefore were protected and no harm could befall them. This was perfectly okay with me, because it was more important that I become their friend than they remain my customers. He accepted the fact that this did not happen to everybody, and that his jinx only existed at Melvyn's.

At one private party we both attended, he broke down and said that both he and his wife thought I had the best atmosphere in town, absolutely loved the place, and did I think that there was a possibility that they could celebrate their anniversary without any service catastrophes. I told him that my personal supervision was no longer enough, and that I would pray to the gods for help.

The following Friday night I watched their table carefully and could not believe my good fortune. Everything seemed to go just fine. I had made a deal with Mr. Grofer that I would not come over to the table until they were ready to leave. As I was watching and feeling a warm glow of success, the "Melvyn's Boys Choir" (a group of waiters and bus boys who sang for special occasions) started singing "Happy Birthday" to them. It was their anniversary!

As they paid their check, they both let out a great sigh of relief, and were grinning from ear to ear as they motioned for me to come over. I stood at their table repeating over and over again, "I told you we could do it—I told you we could do it!" In my enthusiasm, while I was flapping my hand around to make my point more dramatic, you guessed it…I knocked a glass of water right in Mrs Grofer's lap.

I hadn't seen the Grofers for about six months and, by coincidence, discovered that their son was the newspaper delivery boy for my home. If they ever happen to read this story, I want them to know I tried to make amends in my small way. (Do you think a $20 tip per week to a 14-year-old newspaper delivery boy was excessive?)

FREE LUNCH

As usual, I appeared at my restaurant at 7:45 p.m. to do my nightly stint of chatting and smiling at customers. As soon as I entered the door, my Maitre d' informed me that there was a man at the bar who wanted to say 'hello.' The MD mentioned that this man was very important! He owned two race tracks, was very well known, and the Maitre d' inferred he knew him personally. The Maitre d' was an inveterate horse player (which seems to be an occupational prerequisite in the restaurant industry), and knew all the horse owners, jockeys, and trainers who came into the restaurant.

My Maitre d' brought me over to this man sitting at the end of the bar. He was about 55 years old, 5'6", 150 pounds, with a ruddy complexion, and he was wearing a Western tie and boots. I was then introduced to Mr. Tony Alessio, and he informed me that he owned Agua Caliente Race Track in Tijuana, and Ruidosa Downs in New Mexico. Mr. Alessio immediately asked me if I knew who he was, and, of course, I assured him I did. He called me aside and told me he had been with Frank Sinatra the day before in New York (where Sinatra was filming "Contract on Cherry Street") and that Mr. Sinatra insisted he should make it his business to come in and say 'hello' to me. Having met Sinatra on several occasions, when he was a customer of my restaurant, I was very flattered and impressed. This man could have anything he wanted. Any friend of Mr. Sinatra's was certainly a friend of mine. He explained that Mr. Sinatra was flying in from New York on Wednesday for some business and that they would be having lunch at my restaurant. He requested I arrange for a secluded table for Sinatra, Spiro Agnew and himself (this was Monday), as he was thinking of using Mr. Agnew for publicity for his race tracks. I spent the next few minutes assuring Mr. Alessio that they would have total privacy at a secluded table where they would not be overheard, and that I would attend to the arrangement personally. He then said, "Frank told me that you were good people and I am going to do something for you." (By this time I was forbidden to call him anything but 'Tony.')

He proceeded to tell me who he was, how big he was, and that his family was recently written up in Newsweek Magazine, and that he would bring in the article which was outside in his car. He went on to tell me about his brother, who was the subject of the Newsweek article, and in prison for income tax evasion. I was really impressed when he told me that there was a book about his family (which he would give me) and his family was actually considered to be a dynasty going back several hundreds of years — having vast holdings in real estate, banking, etc., both in San Diego and Mexico.

Assuming that I was well-known and a "connected guy" (an expression to describe people who knew gangsters), he dropped every name I ever heard, and then some. Not wanting to confess that I was not as worldly as he might think, I greeted each name with a roar, smiling knowledgeably, and picked every third name to ask, "How the hell is Joe Pineapple?" Some of these names actually sounded familiar from younger days when I read *Crime Does Not Pay* comic books.

At that point I recognized a Damon Runyon-type character (who was a jeweler) being seated in the restaurant. This gentleman never ceased to amaze me as he could pull out $75,000 worth of diamonds from his pockets at any given moment to show his customers. The jeweler also seemed to be very well-known and always ran into people he knew in my restaurant. He had a thick European accent and, to hear him tell it, he sold diamonds to every big name in the world. His office was his pocket. I am not quite sure how big an office it was, but as I said before, what came out of there never ceased to amaze me.

I excused myself from Tony to walk over and greet the jeweler. He invited me to have a drink, which I graciously accepted. We chatted awhile and, just to impress him, I casually mentioned that I had the famous Tony Alessio at the bar. The jeweler said he knew Tony's brother very well because he often visited a friend of his in a little-known jail where Tony's brother also was. I told him that when the opportunity presented itself I would introduce him.

I called the Maitre d' over to tell him I would like to introduce the jeweler to Mr. Alessio. The Maitre d' knew the jeweler from the days he worked at Scandia Restaurant in Los Angeles and they both started discussing how important the Alessio family was. The Maitre d' mentioned in conversation that one of my Mexican waiters had won several thousand dollars on a long-shot daily double at Agua Caliente race track only a couple of months before.

Having the story as an excuse to engage Tony in conversation again, I wandered back to where he was sitting. I told the daily double story to Tony just to let him know I knew everything. He acknowledged he also knew about it. He said he had a "boat" race ("fixed" in street jargon) set up at Ruidosa Downs and was going to cut me in for a piece of the "candy" (easy money). He would give me the name of the horse later. I had heard many stories of opportunities like this, but had never had the occasion to capitalize on one.

Just at that moment, my lady came in and joined me. I was all excited to show off my new-found and illustrious friend. What I love about this business is in the two short years I had been in it, at that time, I had made the acquaintance of many notable celebrities, VIPs and accomplished people. Tony was one more feather in my cap. I introduced my lady to Tony and mentioned that he and I had many important mutual acquaintances.

During the conversation it came up that my lady was from Detroit and Tony started to mention every wiseguy from "Frankie Shotgun" to "Willie the Knife." As fate would have it, my gal had either heard the names before, went to school with one of their relatives, or through mutual friends had met them (not to imply that my lady was in that kind of a crowd, but as you often find, large cities are really small cities when it comes to knowing everyone).

Please understand, basically I was high on the fact that Frank Sinatra had insisted this man should come in to say 'hello' to me, and that this man was obviously a "heavy hitter" (a favorite expression of mine to describe important people). The fact that I was now going to share in a financial windfall was just icing on the cake for another great evening at Melvyn's Restaurant and Lounge.

We were all having a swell time when a young lady approached me to ask if I was the owner. She said that she and her girlfriend had been invited down by some gentlemen to attend a charity event that Frank Sinatra would be headlining but she had forgotten where it was to be and could I help her. Embarrassed not to know about such an important event, I turned to Tony at the bar and asked him if he knew anything about it. He said, "Sure," that it was Wednesday night at the Riviera Hotel which was why he had made reservations for luncheon on that same day. It was a personal charity of Frank Sinatra's and that was why he was flying into town on Wednesday from New York. Seeing how disappointed the girls were that they had the wrong day, Tony immediately bought them a drink.

I left the two ladies, my girl and Tony to chat while I did my nightly tour of the dining room. The two girls had left and Tony was sitting alone with my gal at the bar when I returned. By this time Tony seemed a little high and he called me aside to tell me the name of the horse was Diamond Girl in the sixth race and that I would make a lot of money as odds on the horse was 20–1. Now I have received many tips in my life but never one from the owner of a race track, especially one in "McGoonsville" where you could probably pull anything you wanted. In spite of the above, I am a big boy and not too many people in my life have *handed me money.*

I asked Tony how much I should bet and he, of course, said everything I could. He explained that bookmakers didn't handle such a small track but he was flying back the following day and would place the bet for me. He made me swear not to mention it to anybody. He said that when he came in Wednesday for lunch and handed me an envelope full of money, I should just take it and not say a word. My heart started to palpitate as I considered the possibilities while the calculator in my brain worked at full speed. At no time did I consider the amount I might lose, but only how much I wanted to be in that envelope on

Wednesday. For some reason I figured $6,000 as the right number.

Sport that I am, I ripped out three $100 bills and said, "Here." (Five years before I would have begged, borrowed or stolen to bet as much as I could, but based on all the great tips over the years, I guess I was a little gun-shy.) Tony looked at me and laughed. He said he was betting $100 for the Maitre d' *as a tip!* He belittled me sufficiently enough for me to rip out another two $100 bills. He was still reluctant to accept such a menial wager, but he finally condescended, after I jokingly said it didn't matter how much I won as I would probably just give it to my girlfriend anyway.

Just as I was handing him the money, a local bartender from another hotel came in with his wife. Tony mentioned he was waiting for them and all three went to sit in the Lounge. Of course, I sent over a drink immediately and then took my girlfriend into the dining room to join the jeweler's table.

I told the jeweler the story and that Tony had virtually just handed me $10,000 (20–1 on a $500 bet) and asked the jeweler if things like that really happened? He asked me if I would feel better if he verified Tony's authenticity. I said absolutely and called the Maitre d' over and asked him to find an excuse to introduce my jeweler friend to the "illustrious Mr. Tony Alessio!" The introduction was made in the Lounge. They discussed the little-known jail, the jeweler's friend who Tony knew, Tony's brother and various other things. The jeweler came back to the table and said, "He's real." Whereupon the jeweler pulled out two $100 bills and said, "Here, I want part of your action."

The Maitre d' walked over to the table and said, "Mr. Alessio just bawled me out and said, 'Don't ever introduce me to anybody without my okay.'" (Spoken like a true big shot, I thought, and I was really impressed.) I then explained to my Maitre d' what had transpired and asked him how much of the bet he wanted. He told me Mr. Alessio was already betting $100 for him but he would take $50 more. I went crazy and said, "*You* are the horse player. How can you bet $50 on the horse and I bet $450! (I didn't tell him the jeweler had taken

$200 of my bet.) *You* play the horses, *I don't*, and *you personally know this guy!*" I then told the Maitre d' he had $100 on the horse—he had no choice. So far I was doing better than I ever had before. I bet $500 and already had $300 back.

Just then a good friend of mine walked in—Marc Lawrence. Marc is a very well-known character actor and has played the "heavy" in 200 or more movies. Everybody knows his face but few know his name. Marc's favorite pastime is sitting at the bar and "goofing" on some of the "fabulous characters" that come in. In the short period of time I had known Marc, I had come to consider him a good friend and confidant. Knowing that this new character I had just met was right up his alley, I told Marc the story. I wanted to impress Marc that I knew people of Mr. Alessio's stature and I was anxious to show Tony that well-known people like Marc were in my immediate circle of friends.

About that time, the couple Tony had been sitting with left and he returned to the bar by himself. I told Tony I wanted to introduce him to my friend Marc and he was agreeable. They quickly took to each other and seemed to cement their relationship when they discovered that both knew Lucky Luciano. (If only my friends in Brooklyn could see me now. There were no big names that were not part of my new world. If I say so myself, I have taken the whole "trip" pretty much in my stride. My hat size has only increased three inches!)

After I made the introduction, I wandered over to some other guests at the bar. One gentleman, a nightly two-drink customer, was at the bar and I went over to chat with him. The jeweler came over to say 'goodbye' and, kiddingly, I told him to send an armored car around Wednesday to pick up his winnings. He responded that he had plenty of room in his "office" (his pockets).

Meanwhile, Marc and Tony were having a ball in the bar reminiscing about all the people they knew. I overheard names like Lucky Luciano, Frank Sinatra, Al Capone, plus other assorted characters. As fate would have it, my regular customer, with whom I was sitting, was a personal friend of Mr. Sinatra's and questioned me about the guy at the end of the bar who was dropping names so loudly. Excitedly, I told him the story. He expressed doubt that Mr. Sinatra was going to be in town, and that he had not heard about it, although he admitted it was possible. As he was probably the most negative guy I have ever met, I took his comments in stride. He suggested that I call someone we both knew who was really close to Frank. I called the other man to find out if Frank was expected in town but he also said he knew nothing about any charity event and suggested I call the Riviera Hotel to find out if it was on the schedule. This sounded like a good idea, so I called the Riviera Hotel and they knew nothing about the affair. I insisted there must be some mistake. I finally called the owner of the hotel at home and it took him to convince me there was no such event scheduled.

I was a little confused at this point. I drifted over to Marc and Tony (they were getting along famously) and casually asked Tony if he was sure this charity event was the coming Wednesday. He seemed a little perturbed that I interrupted his new-found "love affair" but assured me it was. Now, even more confused I returned to my negative friend, Herb, and told him what had transpired. He then suggested I find out where Alessio was staying.

In order to get into the conversation with Tony and Marc, I strained my memory for gangsters out of the past so I could join in. When I came up with "Louie the Lip," I was welcome to join in the "nostalgia game." Knowing the answer even before I slipped the question about where Tony was staying, he looked at me surprised at my naivete and said, "I am staying at Frank's, of course!"

I returned to Herb to figure out the next step in my investigation. I must admit that at this point, it all sounded more than a little dubious—mainly because the names he was mentioning are not usually repeated loudly in public. (In my experience, people in that type of circle never drop names, and if they do, they do it very discreetly.)

Herb then told me he had seen Tony paying a check for a $1.50 beer with a hundred dollar bill. It quickly dawned on me it must have been one of the five I had given him. I ran into the dining room, found the Maitre d', and called him into a secret huddle and asked, "Are you sure this guy's Tony Alessio?" He replied, "Before you came in, we chatted awhile and he seems to know all about race tracks and horses, plus you had the jeweler verify him. Why would he try to fool you?"

Really confused at this point, I figured out the best thing I could do would be to have Marc Lawrence verify Tony's authenticity. I ran to an in-house telephone at the back of the Lounge and had Marc paged to the phone so I could tell him of my suspicions. I explained my fears, urging him to test and verify Tony's credibility. I briefly explained what had transpired up to the last few minutes.

Just as I was about to hang up, who comes sauntering over to me but good old Tony Alessio. "Mel, I just wanted to say goodnight and make sure everything is all set for Wednesday." At that point I almost swallowed the phone. I thanked him profusely and assured him I could not wait to see him again. (What an understatement!) As he was walking out of the Lounge, I called the parking lot attendant and told him to write down the license plate number of Tony's car. Two minutes later the attendant called me back to say Tony had not called for a car but was walking off the property. I ran out into the street just as Tony was pulling away in a pick-up truck! I didn't know whether to laugh or to cry.

I went back to the bar, found Marc and reviewed the whole evening. We put our heads together and figured out the horse was not a 20-1 long shot, but that Tony Alessio was.

I must explain here that I have been conned 472 times in my life and for much greater sums of money, but I must admit, I was getting a little tired of this nonsense.

I could not sleep that night as my mind was going a mile a minute reviewing everything that had taken place. I could not wait for morning so that I could start to verify all the questions that were spinning in my mind.

For some reason, I clung to the weakest explanation as being the most significant. (I just couldn't believe that anyone in Palm Springs would have the nerve to throw Frank Sinatra's name around, as this is a very small town.)

The following morning I called Ruidosa Downs to find out they were not even open for two more months. Still hoping against hope, I figured he meant Agua Caliente Race Track and that I had misunder-stood him. I called my Maitre d', woke him up and told him to come right over to the restaurant. He was incredulous when I told him the story, and felt that the confusion was in my mind and that Wednesday we would be rich. We figured our next move should be to contact the local bartender who had been having drinks with Tony Alessio the night before and find out what he knew. After ten phone calls to track him down, he said that he knew this man as Tony Alessio through a customer of his from San Diego. He told me this customer usually had lunch at the place he worked every day at 12:30. Not knowing what else to do at this point, I anxiously waited until the lunch hour so I could find this fellow from San Diego who knew Tony Alessio.

I got to the bartender's place about 12 o'clock to make sure I didn't miss the guy. The bartender told me that the customer had just gone to get a cashier's check to bet on the horse. Mr. Alessio was expected to pick it up. Just then the man who originally introduced the bartender to Tony Alessio came into the restaurant and the bartender introduced me to him. I pounced on the poor guy and started questioning him about Alessio. He explained to me that he owned several restaurants in San Diego and Tony Alessio had been coming into his place for the past six months and that as far as he knew, he was Tony Alessio.

There was nothing more I could do and I am still hoping against hope that it was my mistake and that I misunderstood Mr. Alessio.

We still have his private table set in the corner of Melvyn's in the hope that I did misunderstand him and made the reservation for the wrong date, the wrong week, the wrong month—or maybe even the wrong year!

Postscript: Several months after this incident and by sheer coincidence the real Mr. Tony Alessio checked in to the Ingleside Inn. He read the story and told me that he was well aware of this imposter and knew of several other times that he had done exactly the same thing and had yet to be caught or discovered!

I Failed My Memory Course

Through the first summer during the remodeling, many locals
stopped by the Inn to see what was happening. The word was
all over town that some "slick guy from New York" with
plenty of money had taken it over. I received lots of advice, opinions
and comments. I put together my hotel crew during the month of
September. My staff consisted of a very nice-looking man about fifty
years old whom I had gotten through a hotel agency in Los Angeles
to work the Front Desk. He was an ex-alcoholic who obviously had
gone astray, but was perfect for appearances sake. In addition, there
were two other people at the Front Desk whom I don't even
remember. I managed to get back the original, flower-picking housekeeper. I hired a 60-year-old veteran named Luke as Bell Captain, and
kept Skip and Larry to work with him and do odd jobs. Jay was my
aide-de-camp. My hotel staff was set. I hired a local Maitre d' who had
worked in several of the top restaurants in Palm Springs and he staffed
the dining room.

September was drawing to a close, and the place was looking
pretty good. We were not completely finished, but I had come to the
realization that it would never be completely finished. Charlie, the
chef, had put together a very ambitious menu. We decided to open the
doors on the last Friday of September. I chose not to plan a big
opening, but to sort of open quietly, so that I could iron out any kinks.
I placed a small ad in the local newspaper announcing that Melvyn's
was now serving dinner. I had made up a critique sheet that I was going
to use throughout the first week of operation, in order to get the
customers' reactions. It was presented at every table with the check,
and the waiter was instructed to buy a round of drinks for every table
that filled it out.

As I was driving to the restaurant Opening Night, I had no idea
what to expect. As I walked through the doors, I was surprised to find
the bar full of people and the dining room full. To say I was nervous is
an understatement. The Maitre d' informed me we were sold out.
Wow! I never would have guessed. As I looked around the totally

unfamiliar crowd, it seemed that all the women were beautiful, all the men were great-looking, and that everybody was beautifully dressed. I had argued with myself that day as to whether or not to wear a tie, but luckily had made the right decision to do so. Had I guessed wrong, I would have been totally out of place — all the men were wearing jackets and ties.

The Maitre d' pulled me into a corner in the dining room and gave me a run-down on the people who were there. As he related their names and who they were, I got all the more nervous. It sure seemed like I had the *Who's Who* of Palm Springs. I circulated throughout the dining room and bar for about two hours, having no idea what to do. Several people stopped me as I walked around and introduced themselves and wished me good luck. This was going to be more fun than I thought. I had hired a piano player for the Lounge and he was tinkling in the back, and that area started to fill up with customers.

Over the summer, I had become friendly with a nice young man about nineteen years old who used to come around and offer any help he could. We had just taken a liking to one another. His name was Danny, he was a college student who supported himself by parking cars at a restaurant two blocks away. He had assured me that when I opened he would recommend people come to my place.

That night, several people came in and mentioned that Danny had sent them. About 10 o'clock, I walked outside to have a cigarette, and just at that moment, a motorcycle pulled up with a guy dressed in dungarees and T-shirt and sporting a beard—certainly not the 'Ingleside' type I thought. Seated behind him was a pretty girl, just what I needed. The guy said he had come to see the "new" place. Politely I told him it was opening night and asked him to please come back another time. He smiled at me and simply drove off. I was pleased with myself for handling the situation so adeptly.

About 11:00 p.m., my young friend, Danny, showed up and said, "Mel, have you been getting all the people I've sent over?" I told him I had and thanked him. He asked how I enjoyed meeting Steve

McQueen and Ali McGraw. Startled and disappointed that I had not, I said they hadn't shown. He said he was surprised because they told him that they would go right over and have a drink with me. I assured Danny I would have been told if they had come in. He said, "They were on a big, blue Harley Davidson motorcycle and Steve McQueen was wearing jeans and a T-shirt!" It was only to be the first of many blunders.

One of the biggest assets you can have as a successful restaurateur is a great memory for names. Unfortunately, this quality is not one of my native attributes.

There were four incidents which took place almost immediately that taught me that I couldn't bluff my way through difficult situations.

The first one concerns one of the great names in motion picture history who started frequenting my place right after it opened. He was the legendary Darryl Zanuck. I was very impressed that the legendary Mr. Zanuck had chosen my place as one of his favorites. At that time he was dining in the restaurant regularly, three times a week. Of the many VIPs and celebrities that had come in, I was most impressed by him because he was at the pinnacle of power when I was an impressionable child. So was, I might add, Cecil B. De Mille, and their names to me were almost synonymous. It seemed that whenever I read about one, I read about the other. I often refer to the fact that I was twenty-eight years old before I discovered Ferrante and Teicher were two people, as I always thought it was one guy playing one hell of a piano.

It was probably the twentieth time Mr. Zanuck had come into the restaurant when I walked up to him, extended my arm, and said, "Good evening, Mr. DeMille, how do you feel today?" Without blinking an eye, Mr. Zanuck muttered under his breath, "He's been dead ten years." I tried to pass it off as an intentional joke but got nowhere. It was just one of many embarrassments I was to suffer in my newfound career.

The second incident that sticks in my mind was during one very busy Saturday evening, when a woman whose name I should have known, having chatted with her several times, gave me a big greeting which I returned, avoiding, however, the use of her name. She inquired about my lady's well-being and I told her she would be staying at home that evening. She said, "Please give her my regards." I assured her I would, and went about my wandering. I passed her table again about ten minutes later, and she said, "Please make sure you tell Carol I was asking for her." Again I assured her I wouldn't forget. About an hour and a half later, after the lady had finished her dinner and was leaving the restaurant, she came by to bid me farewell, and for the third time, said, "Now don't forget to tell Carol I was asking for her," and again, I swore on all that was holy I would do it. She looked at me and said, "What is my name?" I stammered, stuttered, faked a coronary, used every ploy imaginable to avoid the embarrassment of confessing the truth. Even now, years later, she never forgets to mention it. However, I have improved in this area considerably. I actually do remember her name…about one-third of the time!

And the third event: it was seven o'clock and I was at home getting ready for a big Saturday night in the restaurant. Saturday nights in Palm Springs restaurants are unique unto themselves. It is basically a Saturday-night town—you do about 60% of your business on that one evening. The phone rang, I answered it, and the voice on the other end of the line said, "Hello, Melvyn, this is Dave Matthews." I recognized the name immediately as being a very substantial and important man in Palm Springs, both socially and in business. I knew I knew him, but for the life of me I could not picture his face. Dave went on to explain that he was embarrassed about the nature of his call and that he had never done this before. He was coming to dinner at my restaurant about eight o'clock with some very important people, and would I be kind enough to make a big fuss over him.

In the two short months I had been in the restaurant business, I'd discovered that as the owner of an "in chic" restaurant, people cultivated your attention and acquaintance. It was a phenomenon that I never quite understood, but I was thoroughly enjoying my new-found position of importance, nonetheless.

There was no doubt that Dave was very uneasy and truly embarrassed. I suppose he felt it would make an impression on his important guests if I really did make a big to-do over him. My mind was racing a mile a minute—I had no idea how to ask him for a way to recognize him. Considering the embarrassment he was already experiencing over asking me this favor, I hated to add to it by asking him how I would recognize him. I was sure it would be the ultimate blow to his ego at that moment.

Anyway, I assured him it was no imposition at all, and that even without his special request, I considered him to be an important enough customer to go out of my way to show him special attention. Ingeniously, I explained that it was always so chaotic on a Saturday night that just to make sure there were no slip-ups in the dark Lounge, amidst masses of people, perhaps he should tell me what he would be wearing. I went on to explain that being new to the business added to my nervousness in facing Saturday night crowds, and people tended to become faceless under those conditions. He said he would be wearing a navy blazer with a white open shirt and a white breast hanky, and would be in a party of six arriving at approximately 8 o'clock.

Not taking any chances, at ten minutes to eight I stationed myself at the end of the bar right near the entrance to the restaurant. Almost at the second of 8 o'clock, the door opened and a party of six walked in. The first gentleman through the door was wearing a navy blazer, white open shirt, and white breast-hanky. Immediately I rushed over to him and said "Mr. Matthews, how great to see you, welcome back," and carried on as if he were God Himself. Quickly the man standing <u>behind</u> the one I was addressing stepped up and in a tone that is difficult to describe said, "Melvyn, <u>I</u> am Mr. Matthews!"

What was he wearing? A navy blazer with a white breast hanky and a white open shirt, the same as the gentleman in front of him.

Suffice it to say that these stories taught me a lesson. Now my standard response is, "Please forgive me, I have met so many people in such a short period of time, I know your face, but for the moment have forgotten your name."

There is no question but that honesty is the best policy.

OLD BLUE EYES

When I first came to live in Palm Springs I was very aware that I lived in the same small town that Mr. Sinatra did. Being in the saloon business, you come in contact with people who know everything going on around town. Mr. Sinatra's comings and goings were everyday conversation. It seemed to make you important just to know that Frank left for Vegas today or, Frank got back in town tonight or, Frank's over at such and such restaurant, etc.

It seemed that Mr. S moved around Palm Springs rather easily and frequented almost all the places. I had a bartender working for me who was the best friend of Mr. Sinatra's valet and that alone made me feel important. Many of my customers had either been to his house or at parties with him. Several times during my first month in business, rumor had it he would be visiting "my store." It hadn't happened and I started to get the feeling it never would.

One night someone from another restaurant called and told me that Mr. S and his party had just left there and were on their way to my place. I figured it was a false alarm. However, about 20 minutes later, three cars pulled up and, lo and behold, in the group was Mr. S 'Himself.' I started to get nervous pangs but relaxed a little when I realized that I knew three of the people in his group. As they entered the restaurant, I ran to the familiar faces and greeted them as if they were long lost relatives. I really cannot describe the feeling, but of all the people I had met, I definitely was in awe of Mr. Sinatra. Much to my surprise, he positioned himself at the front end of the bar, quite accessible to everyone. Customers from the restaurant passed by and glanced at him, but gratefully nobody bothered him. He and his entourage stayed about two hours. My place was now officially on the map.

Over the next few months, Mr. S returned five or six times. I knew he made me nervous because, without thinking, I would wind up in the storage room, the kitchen, the men's room, or any other place that was far away and inaccessible to his party. I was dying to have my picture taken with Frank Sinatra. On one occasion the Maitre d' asked Mr. S if he would be kind enough to have his picture taken with the owner's son and Mr. S was very curt and told him that he didn't take pictures while he was out relaxing. As much as I wanted the picture, I respected the fact that he came to my restaurant as a customer and, if he did not want to be disturbed, that was his right.

Mr. S always came in with a very interesting group of people. And while some members in the group would change occasionally, Barbara Marx was always included (they were not yet married). One of Sinatra's employees informed me very confidentially that Barbara and Frank were planning to get married in four weeks at the Annenberg Estate on a Sunday afternoon. He impressed upon me how confidential this was. There was one thing I didn't want to do and that was to antagonize Mr. S with my big mouth.

The following week Mr. S and his entourage came in and during the course of the evening the manager said Mr. Sinatra would like to see me. I could not believe the butterflies in my stomach. Mr. S was sitting in the back of the lounge by himself waiting for me to join him. As I sat down, he told me he wanted to throw a little dinner party at Melvyn's on a Saturday night. Immediately I realized that it would be the Saturday night preceding the scheduled wedding date and it was going to be, in fact, the pre-wedding dinner. He was meeting with me to make the arrangements. I really had no idea how to set up a party, least of all a special one like this, and was wondering how I was going to bluff my way through.

The first question Mr. S asked was whether we had black or gray caviar. The way he posed the question—I had a fifty-fifty chance of guessing right. Before I could answer, he asked me another question about wine that I had no shot at answering. I saw it as the perfect excuse to suggest that I bring my manager into the conversation so he could help us plan this special occasion. I was absolutely amazed at Mr. S's attention to detail. He knew exactly what he wanted, how it was to be cooked, how it was to be served, even how it was to be positioned on the plate. I could not believe that this giant superstar had the ability or inclination to focus on the minutest of details.

The Saturday night dinner party was to be held in July and I asked Mr. S if he wanted us to close the entire restaurant to the public. He replied that would not be necessary as long as we could assure him there would be privacy for his party. We had a separate patio dining room which we could open to the public and still maintain his privacy in the other two dining rooms. I could not believe this was really happening and that I would actually be having Frank and Barbara Sinatra's pre-wedding dinner at my restaurant. Just the thought of all the world-famous dignitaries and VIPs who would be there was mind-boggling to me. We went over all the details and finalized all of the arrangements.

The three weeks passed rather quickly and all of a sudden it was the night of the big party. I had fortified myself with several shots of whiskey, primarily because the butterflies in my stomach were thirsty. As I waited anxiously by the front door, I saw that the first people to arrive were Ambassador Annenberg and his wife. I had always hoped I would have the honor and pleasure of meeting him as he was one of the world's great philanthropists. The door opened and Ambassador and Mrs. Annenberg entered, but before I could open my mouth, Ambassador Annenberg extended his hand and said, "Melvyn, I've been looking forward to meeting you. I've read so much about you!" You could have knocked me over with a feather! (I guess that's what makes a great diplomat. I have told that story a thousand times. The Ambassador has made an indelible impression in my mind and all it took was one thoughtful statement. There certainly is a lesson there.)

Mr. S had hired his own security to make sure that there would be no intrusions by anybody, especially the press. The party started at approximately 8:00 p.m. At 8:30, three people with cameras slung over their shoulders and looking very suspicious walked up the driveway to the entrance of the restaurant. The security people confronted them and they said that they were from the *National Enquirer* and wanted to take some pictures of the party. I was absolutely shocked that they were so obvious and that they admitted who they were. I wondered how this tabloid ever got any inside stories using this kind of modus operandi. However, that was their business. Needless to say, the security people promptly escorted them off the property.

The patio was jammed with customers as it always was on a Saturday night in Palm Springs. In spite of my nervousness the party went without a hitch and it seemed like everybody was happy. Frank had gifted Barbara that day with a new Rolls Royce which they had driven to the restaurant. I didn't hear one word about the wedding that was to take place the following day. Their party started to break up at one o'clock in the morning and there were still customers sitting on the patio. Frank and Barbara were the last to leave with their friend, Jilly Rizzo. My manager and I walked them out to the car. They thanked us for a lovely evening as the valet brought up the new Rolls Royce.

After Frank and Barbara were securely in their car, my manager and I started to walk back to the restaurant, congratulating each other on getting through the entire evening without a problem. Just then we heard a commotion and turned around to see the Rolls Royce stop in the middle of the driveway and Frank screaming at two men, while Jilly Rizzo was running toward them. There was a camera hanging around one of the men's necks, which Jilly immediately grabbed, opened the camera and took out the roll of film. With that, Frank told Jilly to handle it and drove off. It seems one of the two men was screaming that Frank Sinatra had tried to hit him with the car. Jilly returned to the bar with the manager and I so we could figure out exactly what had happened.

Twenty minutes later Mr. Sinatra was on the phone asking to speak to me. He told me that he had not attempted to hit the two men with the car, but rather when they jumped out from behind a tree and took the picture, the flash temporarily blinded him and the car veered off to the side and, that if police were called, I was to tell them that was exactly what had happened.

What actually had happened was the following. The *National Enquirer* had sent two couples, very well-dressed, to have dinner at Melvyn's. They were seated on the patio. The three people who had shown up earlier were deliberately obvious so that they could be thrown out and everybody would feel safe and secure...they were just decoys. The two couples that had dinner on the patio waited the entire evening until Barbara and Frank were about to leave. Then the men positioned themselves behind a large tree that the Sinatra's would have to drive by in order to leave. They then jumped out from behind the tree, took the picture through the car window from a camera that one of the men kept in his inside jacket pocket. The camera around the neck was a phony because they knew the film would be taken from it. The camera with the actual picture was hidden back in his jacket pocket. The picture of Frank and Barbara in the car appeared in the following week's edition of the *National Enquirer*. I guess they really are good at getting the story.

Several years passed after the wedding and the Sinatras came in occasionally. I had recently turned my insurance business over to a rather prominent broker in the desert. He was personal friends with President and Mrs. Gerald Ford and was going to host a party in honor of their 35th wedding anniversary. As a new client, I was invited to this very auspicious occasion. Boy, was I traveling in the right circles!

I had just met the lady who is now my wife and casually asked her if she wanted to be my date for this party. It was a black-tie affair and, needless to say, very elegant and certainly star-studded.

By this time I knew every photographer in the area and all of them knew I would love to have my picture taken with Frank Sinatra. As my date and I entered the party, the photographer for the evening came up to me and said, "Mel, tonight is the night you're going to be in a picture with Frank Sinatra. Just position yourself next to him and I guarantee you a picture." I was torn between acting cool with my new date and getting a picture with Mr. S. I opted for the picture.

Mr. S casually greeted me as my date and I passed by on the way to the buffet table. I told my date to remain there until I took care of some important business and then proceeded to locate Mr. S. I sort of sashayed next to him, the photographer gave me a thumbs-up sign, and as he went to shoot the picture, Mr. S turned around to greet somebody. Everytime I positioned myself next to him for the photographer Mr. S turned to chat with somebody. *This went on for thirty minutes!* By this time the cat was out of the bag and it was obvious to my lady what my "important" business was. After chasing him like a puppy dog for some time, Mr. S engaged in a conversation with a certain gentleman. The photographer signaled to me where I should stand and as he counted one to three with his fingers, I popped up between them and he snapped the picture. Both Sinatra and the man he was talking to looked at me like I was crazy but had no idea what I had done.

A week later I received the picture and if I had not told you the story you would think that Mr. Sinatra, this gentleman and I had been engaged in a serious conversation! Today the picture proudly hangs in the lounge of Melvyn's.

There are two interesting postscripts I would like to add to my Sinatra vignette.

One: I serve as one of the directors of a local charity, Angel View Crippled Children's Foundation. As such I was to meet with one of the trustees of the Bob Hope Golf Tournament regarding a grant for my charity. As the trustee and I sat down to have lunch at my restaurant, he mentioned that he had a picture of me hanging in his office. Not remembering having met the gentleman before, I was quite flattered, but even more curious as to why he had this picture. He told me it was a picture of me, Sinatra, and himself engaged in conversation at a party. It then dawned on me that even he was convinced that I belonged in the picture and was actually a part of the discussion.

Two: Several years ago, I was contacted by the famous author, Kitty Kelley, and she told me she wanted to meet with me regarding a biography she was doing on Frank Sinatra. I was really quite flattered that somebody thought that I was that close to Mr. S and could recount any stories of significance. Miss Kelley (who incidentally has become world-famous for her stinging biography of Nancy Reagan) and I met and chatted for quite a while. As I told her about events I recalled within my limited contact with the Sinatras, I was totally unaware of the type of book she intended to write and just assumed she was gathering anecdotes from locals regarding their contacts with Mr. Sinatra. Needless to say, there was nothing of any interest that I knew or could tell about the Sinatras. Much to my surprise, when the book came out, my cooperation was acknowledged, along with many others, in the front of the book.

I'm certainly glad she didn't ask me anything about Nancy!

THE RAGS

In 1979 I built a disco called Cecil's which became a real hot club catering to the jet setters, celebrities, and all the various beautiful people. One of the top reporters from one of the tabloid newspapers started hanging around in order to pick up little tidbits about the stars. He made friends with my son, who was working at the club, and made an arrangement to call my son every week to find out what was happening. My son was receiving checks between $100 to $150 every time he told him a cute item. They were harmless little column items and I was enjoying the publicity. On many occasions, the tabloid would exaggerate or embellish the story so that it seemed a lot more sensational than it really was. After my son no longer worked there, the reporter would call me from time to time and if something cute happened, I would tell him. The calls became less frequent after a while, however two particular incidents stand out in my mind.

I received a call from the reporter asking me what I knew about a serious fight that supposedly had taken place between Barbara and Frank Sinatra. I told him I knew nothing about it nor had I heard anything about it. (For some reason Barbara and Frank never called me when these things happened.) The next thing I knew, there were two reporters from the tabloid at the front desk of my hotel. They asked me where they might find the Sinatras and with total authority (like the Sinatras always gave me their schedule) I mentioned the name of another local restaurant where they went on occasion. As fate would have it, the Sinatras were having dinner there that evening and the reporters were thrilled. The following week I received a check from the tabloid for $200 with the stub marked 'Sinatra Story.'

From time to time the reporter would call me primarily to stay in touch. One day the reporter called and asked what I knew about Elizabeth Taylor being in the Betty Ford Center. I said I knew nothing about it. He didn't believe it and tried to cajole me into telling him what I really knew. I repeated that I had no idea what he was talking about and he finally hung up. The next week I received a check from the tabloid for $250 and the stub was marked 'Elizabeth Taylor Story.'

I couldn't imagine what I would get if I actually had known something!

Several years passed and I was no longer the star of the tabloids. It was just as well as I was receiving a lot of good press in various newspapers and magazines for both the restaurant and hotel. I had appeared on several national TV shows and all this publicity played a major part in my success. Because of this it was automatic that anybody with the press occupied a favorite place in my heart and I cooperated with them totally.

One day, I received a phone call from a man with an English accent, who introduced himself as a free-lance writer for several major European magazines. He said he would like to come to the hotel to do a major feature story on the Inn and the Restaurant. I told him I would be happy to work with him. After he arrived and checked in we made an appointment for the following morning at 10:00 a.m. We met the next day and spent about two hours chatting about my background, the history of the Inn , and the success of the celebrity anecdotes. (This always seemed to add spice and notoriety to any story.) I mentioned a few cute incidents —more to drop the names of the famous than to tell anything newsworthy. I told him that the previous week Donald Trump and Marla Maples had come into the restaurant and celebrated Marla's Birthday. I had not been in that evening but my staff had told me how nice they had been and had allowed pictures to be taken with the Maitre d' and others of the staff. They were staying at another local hotel while Marla was doing some TV work in Palm Springs. The writer asked if I had any pictures with celebrities that he might use with his story. He told me that Europeans were in love with American celebrities. I showed him quite a few celebrity pictures on the wall in the back of the lounge. He asked if I would mind if he took them off the wall so he could photograph them to use with his story. I told him to feel free to use whatever he liked. He assured me he would replace them. He checked out late that afternoon after thanking me for the time I spent with him. He assured me that I would receive copies of the articles as soon as they were published.

About two months passed and a friend called and asked what I thought about the story in one of the 'rags.' I asked him what story he was talking about, and he said that his friend just called him from Michigan and mentioned that there was a two page story about me with eight different pictures of me with various celebrities. I immediately sent one of my people to the local supermarket to pick up a copy of the tabloid. I was absolutely flabbergasted! I read the story and felt absolute panic. The headline read: *"Owner of Desert Love Nest Spills the Beans on Stars Raunchy Romps!"*

The story allegedly quoted me telling stories about eight different major celebrities. I was absolutely shocked! Sure enough, there were eight different pictures in the article of me with various celebrities. They all had one thing in common, they were all pictures that were hanging on the wall in the back of the lounge. All of a sudden it dawned on me that the culprit was the free-lance English writer as he was the only one who had ever taken pictures of those photos. Plus, he wrote about Donald and Marla who had only been there a short time before. The story quoted me as saying that Donald Trump and Marla Maples hardly ever left their suite and that they only seemed to come out of their room for meals (implying that they made love all day.) The truth was I had told him that they didn't even stay at my hotel and that I never even met them personally. He had taken some harmless little anecdotes and twisted them and exaggerated them until they had a dirty, sensationalist twist to them.

I cannot accurately describe how I felt. I felt betrayed, deceived, embarrassed, mortified and furious all at the same time. I started getting calls from friends, customers and various press wanting to know my reaction to the story. I refused to discuss it, and simply said it was all lies and made believe that if I ignored it, it would go away. I actually felt threatened that a story like that could ruin my business. The first thing you learn in a business that caters to high profile people is that you don't tell stories about them and I hadn't! The whole story he wrote was contrived in his imagination and only substantiated by the photos he copied from the wall!

I explored the possibility of a lawsuit but my attorney advised me that it would call even more attention to the article. His advice was to 'let sleeping dogs lie!' This story was written two months after the publication of the "Rag Story" and fortunately, I haven't heard much about it in the last month.

So, number one: You don't have to be a celebrity to suffer at the hands of the 'Rags' and; number two: you can bet I will check credentials *very carefully* before I give another interview!

HERE, THERE, EVERYWHERE...

He came in to the restaurant several times. He looked very eerie. He would walk all around, look in every corner, never talk to anyone and leave. With each visit he became more obvious. He never came with anyone, and he never as much as bought a drink.

One evening, as I was chatting with another local restaurateur, he walked in. The other restaurateur said, "So he comes in to your restaurant too!" I asked if he knew him. He said all he knew was that his name was Jerry and it was rumored that he worked for the IRS. He said he had been coming into his restaurant for about two years and behaved exactly the same way in his restaurant. Jerry never spoke to anybody, never spent any money, just came in and walked around to see who was there and left.

Over the next year, whenever I attended a major charity function, sure enough, Jerry would be there lurking around. Whenever he would come into my restaurant I would make him a topic of conversation and several customers mentioned that they had seen him at many different places. One customer mentioned that Jerry was an attorney from Chicago, who had made a life's work of being at the "in places" at the "right time." He also said that he heard that Jerry had crashed a party at Frank Sinatra's house, was thrown out ten times, but finally on the 11th attempt, Sinatra said let him stay.

One Saturday, a group of friends and I bought tickets to watch a championship heavyweight title fight on a private TV cable system at a local hotel. As we were waiting for the fight to begin the TV cameraman panned the ringside seats, and who was sitting in one of the best seats ringside? None other than Jerry!

One time, my manager and I were invited to a customer's home to attend a VIP party during the Bob Hope Classic Golf Tournament. The guest list included President and Mrs. Ford, Ginger Rogers and other notable people. It was an outdoor luncheon, served on the patio of their home which faced onto a prestigious country club, where we watched the celebrity golfers play as they passed by. As my manager and I were being introduced to the various guests, working our way to the outside patio when, lo and behold, who was standing there by himself in a corner, none other the Jerry. Up to that point we had never spoken even though we had nodded to each other. Curious, I walked over to Jerry and asked, "How do you manage to be at all these places?" Jerry simply replied, "How do you manage to run a restaurant?" I asked him what that meant and he said, "You choose to run a restaurant as a vocation and I choose to go to openings, parties, and important events as my vocation." (Made sense I guess.)

Several months later, my wife and I joined some friends in San Francisco to attend the Super Bowl. As we were unpacking in the hotel room I flipped on the TV. A reporter was interviewing a 'man in the street' about the Super Bowl and guess who was staring at me from the screen? You've got it, our boy Jerry!

Over the next few years, Jerry and I became friends and I always enjoyed his visits. He would tell me everything that was happening all over the country; who was eating where, which restaurants were closing, which were opening, etc. Jerry had even been on the mountain in Aspen when "the Donald" Trump had the notorious fight with Ivana…he told me about it before it even was in the papers.

One day I received a call that required an unexpected trip to New York. Jerry had just left Palm Springs after attending the 'Skins' Golf Tournament. That night I jumped on the "redeye" flight to New York, arrived at 6 a.m., took care of some business and arranged to meet some of my longtime friends at noon at a new hot restaurant in Manhattan. As I opened the front door to enter, who was standing there…my new, best friend Jerry!

After being friendly with Jerry for about eight years, listening to his stories and observing his lifestyle, I think he may know something that we don't!

P.S. As of this writing there have been several newspaper articles about Jerry as well as a five page article about his exploits in *Chicago Magazine*. He has now become something of a celebrity himself…but, has yet to buy a drink!

THE REAL PHANTOM

According to the dictionary, the word phantom means: "A spectre, an immaterial form, a deceitful appearance, a show without reality."

It was finally the day of the big event! We had contracted a professional theme party company to stage *The Phantom of the Opera* at Melvyn's Restaurant. We were very excited and had spent a lot of money and energy promoting the evening. We had printed tent placards for the restaurant's tables and put them out six weeks before the show. We had printed 5,000 newsletters which we mailed and distributed every place we could think of. We even advertised the exciting event on outdoor billboards. (One billboard was so effective that I received a phone call from a doctor who told me that he was so mesmerized by the billboard that he rear-ended the car in front of him. He called to suggest that I tone it down since several friends of his mentioned that they too almost had accidents while reading the sign. I guess that kind of attention is the ultimate compliment for a billboard campaign.)

We had produced two other very successful promotions: A Night with the Kingston Trio and a Murder Mystery Night. Our customers had asked for more special events. When we originally met with this particular party company, they offered us a variety of theme parties but the *Phantom* seemed just perfect for Melvyn's. They described how beautifully they would decorate the room, simulating an opera house, and how "the Phantom" and Christine would stroll around and sing songs from the magnificent score. We agreed on a date and told them to draw up the contract. We were ready and anxious to go. My manager and I calculated that we would have to charge $100 per person (which made me a little bit nervous, even though I knew the value would be there) to cover the cost of production, the advertising and promotion, and a six-course gourmet meal (tax and tip included).

As the weeks passed, it became quite a topic of conversation and we were getting a satisfactory amount of reservations. The room we chose for the performance only held about 80 comfortably. It took an inordinate amount of time to get the bios of the performers so that we could send out publicity releases. They finally arrived (without accompanying photos) and when the local newspapers received the notices, the entertainment editor personally called me to say that he knew of these particular singers and that we were lucky to get such great talent.

Three days before the affair, I received an express mailed letter from a New York law firm with ten names on the letterhead. (I knew ten names meant trouble, nine might not be too bad!) In essence, the letter said that they heard (in New York?) that we were producing *The Phantom of the Opera* and that they represented the people who owned the rights to it. Briefly, they said that either we cancel it or they would serve us with an injunction. Panicky, I called the party company only to be reassured that they had done the *Phantom* before and there absolutely would be no problem. Not wanting to take a chance on a legal problem, my manager called the New York firm and assured them that we were not doing the complete production and that we had paid our BMI and ASCAP fees which gave us a right to perform the music publically.

The affair was scheduled for 6:30 p.m. on a Sunday evening in May. That morning, a lady in town who also does theme parties, happened to be eating in the restaurant and came over to tell me how lucky I was to get these particular singers. She said she had worked with them before and they were really great. She did express surprise that they were available as she thought they were performing on the road. She said that they must have had a cancellation and that's probably why they were available to do this show.

At 4:30 p.m., Sherry, the woman in charge of the production, arrived in a Rolls Royce with a trunk full of decorations. Behind her was a truck full of more decorations and a whole crew to decorate the restaurant. With not a minute to spare, at exactly 6:30 p.m. the restaurant was decorated and truly looked like an opera house. It was beautiful to behold. Every table had a black tablecloth, the chairs were covered in black, the centerpieces were masks from *The Phantom*, every placesetting had a rose and a rolled up scroll of music from the show. The front entrance had a red carpet with Roman columns leading into the dining room. As you drove up, you saw a big gondola and directly in front of the restaurant was a huge pipe organ. If the performance was anything like the decorations, my guests were in for a treat!

The guests started to arrive and some were dressed as if they were going to a real opera. One gentleman was even wearing white tails! It was truly exciting as the trio of musicians started to play. As we started to serve the first course, the musicians were playing regular lounge music. I asked Sherry why the music was not related to *The Phantom* and she replied that they were saving that music for the show. She made a point of telling me that the musicians had rehearsed the score until 2:30 a.m. the previous morning. I asked about the singers and she said they had just arrived and were changing into costume.

At about 7:30 p.m., a man dressed in a tuxedo came out, walked up to the piano, looked like he was going to sing, mumbled one line, and disappeared. Not quite sure what that meant, I sought out Sherry to find out. She said that was not the real singer and that the real singers had been delayed but would be there shortly. She told me not to worry—everything was under control. In spite of the fact that the musicians were very entertaining, we still had not had a hint of the *Phantom* or its music and it was now approaching 8:30 p.m.

My manager and I chased down Sherry again. (This time we found her standing in the street.) She told us she was watching for the singers. It was obvious that the guests were starting to get restless. I asked Sherry to please take the microphone and explain the situation to the guests which she said she would do, but did not.

About 9 p.m., the front desk clerk of the hotel called to tell me that the lady who was running the affair (Sherry) was using the phone in the lobby and he had overheard her desperately calling several different singers and begging them to come to Melvyn's immediately. My desk clerk also told me that there was somebody in our accounting office making copies of the sheet music from *The Phantom of the Opera*.

At this point, I went over to the musicians and begged them to please play something from the *Phantom* until I could find out what was happening. They told me that *they did not know* the music! I ran to the office to confront Sherry. On the way, I encountered a man walking back and forth on the veranda, dressed in a tuxedo, mumbling to himself. I asked him who he was and what he was doing. He replied that I should leave him alone as he was trying very hard to learn the words to a song from *The Phantom of the Opera!*

Another ten minutes passed and finally the man who was trying to learn the words appeared in the restaurant and started to sing one of the songs from *The Phantom* from the sheet music, a cappella (because the musicians did not know the music and could not accompany him). He got halfway through the song when he simply threw down the sheet music and walked out. Sherry came over and said she would do the performance herself and to just give her ten minutes to change into her costume. Twenty more minutes passed and she was nowhere to be found!

Just then a local singer who had worked for me on previous occasions showed up and told me that Sherry had called her in a panic and she decided to run over to do anything she could to help. She said she couldn't do *The Phantom* without the musicians but she would entertain the best she could.

By this time, several customers had walked out vowing never to return to Melvyn's and adding that the whole evening was a scam. I took the microphone at this point and, to the best of my ability, tried to explain what was going on (in spite of the fact that I had no idea what was going on!). I apologized profusely for the disappointment, and pathetically tried to explain that I was as bewildered as they were. (Actually the entertainment, although not from *The Phantom*, was actually quite good, the food was excellent and many people were really having a good time.)

In order to make up for the problem I invited everybody to return for dinner as my guests at their convenience. Most of the customers actually felt sorry for me! At 1:00 a.m., a truck pulled up to retrieve all the beautiful decorations but absolutely no sign of Sherry. As always, thank God, the night finally came to an end and the nightmare was over. Three attempts to reach Sherry the next day failed.

About ten days later I received a phone call from a gentleman who said he would like to see me regarding *The Phantom* evening. He told me that he was the man, according to the press releases, that was supposed to have performed. As a singer, he had done *The Phantom* many times. However, he had been on the road in Canada for the last four months and knew nothing about it. He had never even been contacted about doing it. When he got back to the States, several people he knew called him and asked him why he had not shown up at the performance. When he finally understood the details of what they were talking about, he contacted the woman who was to have performed as Christine only to find out that she was in the dark also. It turned out that the entertainers we were told would perform *The Phantom* had never even been contacted.

We filed a lawsuit against the party company, but to no avail, because shortly thereafter they filed for Chapter Eleven bankruptcy.

Webster is absolutely right to define phantom as "a show without reality."

SERVES ME RIGHT

Mr. Sydney Sheldon

The Palm Springs City Council started a tradition of putting the names of stars in the sidewalk of Palm Canyon Drive (the main street in town), similar to what's done in Hollywood. They had decided to honor the famous author, Sydney Sheldon, with a star. Mr. Sheldon was a regular customer of Melvyn's Restaurant and an employee suggested that, in honor of the occasion, I should invite Mr. and Mrs. Sheldon to dinner as my guests following the ceremony. I agreed and immediately sent out a personal invitation.

The next day, the Maitre d' informed me that Mr. Sheldon's secretary had called and made a reservation for a party of *twenty people* the night of the award (talk about taking advantage!). I spent the next two days muttering to myself. I was actually in a state of shock, but after considering all the possibilities, I realized I had no choice but to be gracious about such a large response to my invitation. My only dilemma was whether or not to fire the employee who had had the brilliant idea to begin with.

As I was opening the mail a couple of days later, just about the time my cheap palpitating heart was calming down, I saw an envelope and couldn't believe my eyes. There before me was my envelope with the invitation addressed to Mr. Sydney Sheldon, returned and unopened because I had sent it to the *wrong address!*

MY IDOL

One day, one of the bellmen rushed up to me excitedly and informed me that Marlon Brando had checked into the hotel. Now, for various reasons, we common folk tend to idolize different movie stars. Marlon Brando is my movie idol. He was a super star during my impressionable, formative years and, in my eyes, he could do no wrong!

We had the honor of having Mr. Brando with us for three days, most of which were cloudy, and most of which he spent in his camper parked behind the Inn on a CB radio talking to everybody. Knowing the people had no idea they were speaking to Marlon Brando on their ham radios, I couldn't help but wonder how different the conversations would have been if they had known they were talking to one of the greatest actors of all time.

During my first few years of owning the Ingleside Inn, I had accumulated a collection of books either written by, or about, guests of the restaurant and/or hotel. I had gotten many of them autographed and, although not a collector by nature, I take great pride in this collection. Realizing the opportunity of adding Brando's autograph, I hurriedly asked the bellman to run to the local bookstore and pick up any book on Brando in stock. Since I was shy about approaching a VIP directly, I asked the bellman if he would please explain my collection of books to Mr. Brando, and ask if he would be kind enough to autograph the book for me. The bellman informed me that he was currently working on a room service order for Mr. Brando and that would be the perfect opportunity.

I waited impatiently and anxiously for about 30 minutes when I finally saw the bellman approaching my office, book in hand. All excited, I asked him if obtaining Mr. Brando's autograph was a fait accompli. To my horror, he told me that Mr. Brando, upon seeing the book grew angry, muttered something under his breath, and almost ripped it up. The book the bellman had purchased, *Brando for Breakfast*, was a very unflattering book written by his ex-wife Anna Kashfi, in which she tore my idol apart.

To this day, I am not sure whether that incident had anything to do with Mr. Brando checking out two hours later.

The ostensible salvation of this whole episode was that the evening before, Mr. Brando had been gracious enough to pose for a picture with me in the restaurant. I was most excited about this opportunity and even had the Maitre d' take three shots in case one didn't come out. Needless to say, the next day we found out there was no film in the camera!

To sum up — no book, no picture, no more Brando. It was par for the course again for Mel Haber!

BETTER LATE
THAN NEVER

While we are on the subject of my book collection, one other anecdote comes to mind. I had just finished reading a book by Paul Erdman, named *The Crash of '79*, and was very impressed with it.

A friend of mine stopped into my office one day to say hello. He asked if I had read any good books lately. I mentioned *The Crash of '79*, said I'd enjoyed it tremendously and recommended it to him. To my delight, he said that he knew Paul Erdman personally. I asked, "As long as you know Paul Erdman personally, would it be possible to get his book autographed for me?" He replied, "Let's call him right now." He pulled out his phone book and called Paul Erdman in northern California. After exchanging hellos, my friend explained to Erdman that I was his friend, had a book collection and asked if he would be kind enough to autograph the book for me. He then put me on the telephone with Mr. Erdman. I explained the situation to him and he said he'd be more than happy to autograph the book if I would send it to him. I put a little personal note in the book and mailed it out UPS that same day. *The book never came back*. There really wasn't too much I could do about it.

As fate would have it, three years later, I was informed that Mr. Paul Erdman had checked into the Ingleside Inn and was out at the pool. I ran out to the pool, introduced myself and said jokingly, "Mr. Erdman, if you didn't want to autograph the book that was okay, but at least give me my book back!" He didn't know what I was talking about so I recounted the story to him. He was really embarrassed because he had no more copies of the book. I tried my best to put him at ease and we both enjoyed a laugh over the incident.

Much to my surprise, Mr. Erdman called me the next day and asked me to come to his room. Unbeknownst to me, he had gone to all the local bookstores to find the book in hardcover so he could autograph it for me, but could not find one. Subsequently, he found a paperback copy of the book which he autographed and gave to me. Mr. Erdman felt so bad that he put me on his publisher's complimentary book list so that every time he comes out with a new book, I receive a complimentary copy directly from the publisher.

Definitely one of my better experiences.

NO LIMIT ON HUMILITY

One day while walking through the restaurant, a friend of mine, who had once been mayor of Palm Springs, called me over to the table to say hello and introduce me to the man with whom he was having lunch, Kirk Kerkorian, the famous entrepreneur.

I had begun accumulating a collection of books about or by people whom I had met through Melvyn's or the Ingleside Inn. I had always been a voracious reader. Generally speaking, I read only non-fiction and biographies. As fate would have it, I had just finished the biography titled, simply, Kerkorian.

I decided to dash home (only about 12 blocks away) to see if I could get the book and be back before they finished lunch. I made it just as my friend and Mr. Kerkorian were having their dessert. I explained to Mr. K about my collection and asked if he would be kind enough to autograph the book for me. He looked at me quite surprised, hesitated a moment and finally asked what I wanted written in the book and I said simply, "To my friend, Mel and just sign your name." He seemed rather unsettled about the whole situation but signed the book nonetheless.

Approximately one month passed and Mr. K was back having dinner with the famed attorney, Greg Bautzer. It was a very busy Saturday night, you could hardly walk through the restaurant, when my manager made his way over to me and said that Mr. Kerkorian wanted to see me. The manager said it seemed to be a matter of importance.

Nervous that the food or the service had been unsatisfactory, I fought my way through the jammed lounge to the front where Mr. Kerkorian was waiting by the exit. I inquired if everything had been satisfactory. He immediately responded, "Mel, the last time I was in you embarrassed me." I was totally taken aback and shocked. I searched my mind frantically for what had transpired the previous time he had been in. I could think of nothing significant and very humbly inquired what I had done. Mr. K said, "Don't you remember? You embarrassed me by asking for my autograph." I was sure he was putting me on. And as I looked into his face, much to my shock, I realized he was dead serious. Suddenly feeling relieved that this was the extent of the damage I had done, I said, "Mr. Kerkorian, do you have any idea who you are?" It dawned on me that he really felt he was not worthy of somebody asking him for his autograph. Talk about humility.

Over the next several months, Kirk Kerkorian stayed in the hotel several times. One day the front desk clerk informed me that MGM studios had called to make a reservation for Kirk Kerkorian's son for the coming weekend. I was flattered that the Kerkorian family was making the Ingleside Inn their headquarters in Palm Springs.

That Saturday evening in the restaurant, several of my customers informed me that they had just met Kirk Kerkorian's son who seemed to be very friendly and outgoing and was socializing at the bar. I asked the Maitre d' to point him out to me and went over and introduced myself. I inquired as to his father's well-being and he told me his dad was in London but he had been told that if he went to Palm Springs the only place to stay was the Ingleside Inn. Boy, did that make me feel great. I asked him what he was doing in town and he told me that he was checking on the Canyon Hotel as a possible business deal for his father. (The Canyon Hotel, a rather large property for sale, had been closed for about a year.) I told him to feel free to contact me and if there was any way I could help him, I'd be more than happy to do so.

The next day, while driving down Palm Canyon Drive with my wife, I stopped at a traffic light. Lo and behold, in the car next to me was George Beebe, the man who originally had brought Kirk Kerkorian into my restaurant. I leaned over and quite proudly yelled to George that I had Kirk Kerkorian's son staying in the hotel. George leaned over and yelled back, "That's great Mel! Kirk Kerkorian *has no son!*" I couldn't believe I had been had again! I immediately drove to the Inn to see if he was still there only to find that he had already checked out signed the bill for $750 and left instructions to bill MGM Studios. Of course I knew the answer before we even called Monday morning and the studio confirmed that Kirk Kerkorian had no son and they knew nothing about any reservation for the Ingleside Inn.

Ho hum, just another one for the book.

THE HUSTLER

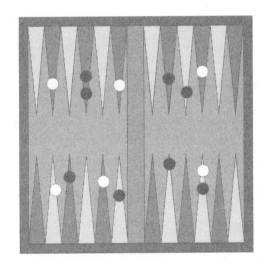

I learned to play backgammon in the late 1960's. It was the "in" game at that time and every chic private club had a backgammon room. Although the game had been played for centuries in the middle east, it had just become the rage in the U.S. I don't remember who originally taught me how to play but everyone I knew was either playing or learning to play. It was an exciting game and played by the affluent at tournaments held in the glamour spots of the world such as Acapulco, Aspen, Monte Carlo, the Bahamas, etc. It is a very high stakes gambling game, primarily because it is played with a "doubling cube" which very quickly multiplies the amount you are playing for. In addition, a "gammon" or "backgammon" doubles or triples whatever is on the doubling cube.

In 1979, I built a very elegant disco/restaurant in Palm Springs and the first thing I did was to create a backgammon area. It was a big attraction and customers played for hours. I personally loved it and played every night. I acquired a reputation as a fairly good player and everybody wanted to take on "the boss." The truth of the matter is that on a scale of ten I was probably a seven-and-a-half. I have always described myself as the 'king of mediocrity.' I did almost everything well but nothing great. I would get to a certain point, be it skiing, playing piano, ice skating, (writing?) and would lose interest and go on to something else.

Everybody wanted to play me for big stakes, but I had no interest in taking their money. I didn't think it would be good for business or my reputation, and I certainly didn't want to lose any serious money. (When I was younger, I went through a gambling stage and was pretty happy that I had finally outgrown it. Many of my friends did not.) I enjoyed having a few drinks when I played which induced me to take a lot more risks in the game. To tell the truth my adrenaline flowed when I played, as if I was playing for my last dollar, no matter what the stakes were! People would actually line up to play me and there were many nights that I was called at home to find out what time I would be at work, so they could be first in line to play me. Many was the night I got so involved that when I left the club the sun was shining and it was 7 a.m. in the morning

One evening I was sitting at the bar, when a very shabbily dressed young man with an equally dressed young lady (I guessed they were in their late twenties) walked over to the bartender near where I was sitting and asked if the owner was in.

I introduced myself and the young man said he was from out of town and looking for a backgammon game. He had heard that I liked to play. Not knowing if I wanted to get involved I asked him what kind of stakes he played for. He said he normally played for $10 a point. I must tell you that that can get quite expensive. The whole scene seemed like a movie where the pool hustler comes into town and wants to take on everybody and anybody.

It was a slow night and I figured I'd kill some time so I agreed to play him for $5 per point. His girlfriend sat next to him, he ordered a drink for her, and we started to play. We started about 10 p.m. I was drinking pretty good (or bad, depending on your perspective), feeling no pain. At midnight, all of a sudden, his girlfriend said she was sleepy and wanted to go home. I looked at the score and I was losing $2,200! I couldn't believe it. I had been set up like a lamb going to slaughter. I said, "No fair, you just can't quit when you are winning, we never established a quitting time." (For those who are not familiar with the ways of gambling, it is typical for the winners to call it quits while the losers are begging for more time!) Much to my surprise, he didn't bat an eye and replied, "Ok, lets play another hour and a half till—1:30 a.m." He told his girlfriend to go and sleep in their truck.

We played for another hour and a half. God must have been watching over me because not only did I win back the $2,200 but at 1:30 a.m. I was ahead by $1,800. He said he wasn't sure he had that much cash with him but if not, I could hold his watch until he came back the next day with the money. I could not believe what a fool I was. I could have lost and paid thousands to this stranger who didn't know if he had $1800. It seemed to me that I really wasn't getting any smarter as I got older. We walked out to his truck together, where his girlfriend was asleep. He woke her and asked her for his wallet. He started counting the cash and he did have the $1800. He handed the money to me very casually and said he had to get his girlfriend home but he'd see me again sometime.

As I drove home through the dark deserted streets at 2 a.m. I felt sure he was going to jump out of somewhere and hold me up. The whole thing just didn't seem right. The following evening, at about the same time, the same fellow and his girl came in again and asked if I wanted to play. Since it was a very active Saturday night and I was really too busy to play, I explained the situation and begged off. He said no problem, that he enjoyed last night and hoped we could do it again some time. I never saw him again!

A Chief Executive Officer of a major corporation became a friend of mine while patronizing my various restaurants. He was a real character and I very much enjoyed his frequent visits. He once told me that he would love to learn to play backgammon. I told him that I really didn't have the patience to teach him. On his next visit he told me that he had found somebody in his home town to teach him and he was getting pretty good at it and couldn't wait to take me on!

Over his next few visits we played a few times and he definitely was learning the game and becoming quite adept at it. One day he called me from Detroit and said he was coming out for a week and was looking forward to playing some serious backgammon with me. It is the kind of game that can become an obsession. I was at the height of my passion for the game, so I could relate to the fact that he had caught the "bug."

Steve arrived on a Monday and we played all day Tuesday with no major decision (money wise), although we were playing for decent stakes. Wednesday, after a long session of playing I lost $5,000 and was very upset about it. Much to my surprise, Steve eagerly took my money and tried to console me by telling me he had just beaten a member of his country club for $25,000. He was really out for blood. I was as shocked by my naivete as I was to realize that he really wanted to take my money. (Granted, I knew we weren't playing for make-believe, but if I had beaten him for $5,000 I would have settled for half. I really just played for the enjoyment).

Thursday we didn't play, but on Friday we did sit down to play again. We started playing at 5 p.m. and finished up at 6 a.m. the following morning. Lo and behold, I was ahead $20,000. We were both wrecked from the long session and all the drinking we had done, and agreed to meet the next evening in my restaurant.

When I awoke, I thought about the night before and the size of Steve's debt. I decided such a large amount of money was pretty serious and I would let him decide how much he thought was fair to pay me. In my mind I decided I would settle for fifty percent, or $10,000. Steve was sitting in front at the bar when I walked in that night. I said, "Steve, I really don't expect you to pay the whole $20,000. What do you think is fair?" With no hesitation Steve said, "How about $3,000?" I couldn't believe it. I said, "Steve, I paid you $5,000 a few days ago— no questions asked because I lost it to you. But you want me to have a net loss of $2,000 after I beat you for $20,000?" End of the story was I settled for $6,000 for a net gain of $1,000. I really didn't care about the amount but it sure made me feel like a sucker. Believe it or not, when Steve visits he doesn't understand why I don't play anymore.

Several years passed, I had sold the club, and hadn't played backgammon in a long time. One evening, a local guy I knew, asked me to join him and his friend at their table. He introduced me to the young man with him and told me that his young friend was staying in the best suite in my hotel. We chatted for awhile when the young man mentioned that he had heard that I liked to play backgammon. I told him that I hadn't played in a couple of years and was not really great even in those days. He invited me to come to his suite to play a few games. I thanked him but begged off saying I was really too busy.

We conversed a bit and he informed me that he was a collector of Peter Max artwork and that there was a piece in the restaurant boutique that he was interested in. He told me that the price on the piece was $6,000 and suggested we play backgammon for the artwork—$6,000 or nothing. Without even thinking I said, "If I was interested, it would be double or nothing." (In other words, $12,000 or nothing.) Without hesitation he said, "OK, let's play for the picture, $12,000 or nothing." I looked over at the guy who introduced us to see if this fellow was good for $12,000 and he nodded affirmatively. Now, it sounded interesting.

I was partners with the man who ran the boutique and called him to explain the proposition and find out how much money he had invested in the Peter Max. He told me that he had owned it for ten years and had originally paid $1,500 for it. I asked if he wanted to go partners with me on the gamble and he said absolutely. We both figured 8-to-1 odds was worth a shot regardless of how bad I was or how good Steve was.

Well, ladies and gentlemen, I made a hotel customer a very happy man that evening with a free Peter Max painting. I still can't accept that I only lost $750 (my half) because in my mind I lost $6,000. I doubt that any other hotelier would go this far for a customer!

MY LITERARY CAREER

B
ecause I didn't know anything about what I was doing, I had plenty of time to dwell on the interesting and different experiences I was having as the operator of an elegant hotel and restaurant. Because I thought these experiences were so unusual and interesting, I would dictate them into a little recorder and have a secretary type them up. I titled the collection *The Ingleside Inn Bedtime Stories* and put them on the nightstands of the hotel rooms. Our guests have enjoyed them; *Palm Springs Life Magazine* even published one of them, and as a result I have been motivated to add more stories.

In January, 1977, I officially became the first victim of a "Lee Marvin Lawsuit." The previous month, December of 1976, the California Supreme Court handed down what became known as The Lee Marvin Decision. As a matter of fact, I, Melvyn Haber, invented the word "palimony." It originally came about as the result of a telephone interview I had with an L.A. Magazine reporter. They were doing their first article on this law and the fact that my suit, being the first lawsuit of that type filed in the courts, prompted them to contact me. The reporter asked me that if payment for divorce was alimony then what would I call payment for a live-in girlfriend? Without thinking, I replied, "Palimony." Immediately recognizing the fact that I had just created "gold," I attempted to register the word with the Screen Writers Guild only to be told I needed a title; whereupon I sent them a title, only to be told I needed an outline; whereupon I sent them an outline, only to be told that I needed something else and, in total frustration, I simply sent myself a registered letter stating that on that day I invented the word "Palimony." (To this day that envelope is still in my safety deposit box).

As a result of my palimony lawsuit, I was invited to appear on several regional television talk shows. Much to my surprise — and I guess everybody else's — I was quite articulate and eloquent on the subject (and obviously humble I might add!). I guess this was because I was so personally involved in the issue. It was definitely an interesting issue to discuss. It got to the point where I was spending a great deal of time doing telephone interviews with various radio stations throughout the country, and traveling back and forth to Los Angeles to do different television shows.

I had not seen the *Phil Donahue Show* at that point in time but I had read an article about it in *People Magazine*. It was a Tuesday and I had just finished taping a *Steve Edwards Show* segment that was to air the following Friday in Los Angeles. Having read that the *Donahue Show* got involved in controversial topics, I told my Gal Friday to call the *Donahue Show* people and ask them to watch the *Steve Edwards Show* on Friday to see if they might be interested in doing something on palimony. After several phone calls, my gal informed me that the *Phil Donahue Show* emanated from Chicago (I had assumed L.A.) and I promptly said, "Then forget about it."

That Friday afternoon at approximately three o'clock (three hours after the *Steve Edwards Show* had aired), the switchboard from the hotel put through a call to my home stating Gail Steinberg from the *Phil Donahue Show* was on the line. Assuming this was a put-on, I told the operator to put the call through and, in a joking way, said, "Hello, when do you want me in Chicago?" The voice at the other end said, "Monday, so we can tape the show on Tuesday." Immediately realizing this might be genuine, I said, "Let's start over. Who are you really and what is this all about?" The lady at the other end of the line informed me that they had watched the *Steve Edwards Show* that day and became interested in having Marvin Mitchelson, the attorney, and me on their show. They said they would pay my air fare to Chicago and put me up in a hotel for the one night. (Marvin Mitchelson had appeared with me on the *Steve Edwards Show*.)

On the following Monday, I flew to Chicago and checked into the hotel where they had made arrangements for me. I received a phone call from the show informing me that they would have a limousine at the front of the hotel at 8 a.m. the following morning with fresh coffee and doughnuts for the ride to the studio. (Quite right! Exactly the way an up-and-coming media star should be treated!) The following morning I arrived at the studio and taped the *Phil Donahue Show* where Mr. Mitchelson and I debated the issue of palimony. I must say that when the program started off, the conservative midwestern audience wanted to lynch me as a womanizer, but I finished my part of the program with a round of applause and the support of the audience. After the show, one of the producers told me that the show aired live only in Chicago. He then gave me the schedule of when it would appear in various other cities across the country.

I was now ready for my luxurious limo ride back to the hotel. I felt like a conquering hero — having turned the "tough" Chicago audience completely around. When I inquired as to where I would find my limo, I was told it was unavailable and the producer asked if I wanted them to call a cab for me. The hotel was approximately twenty miles away and I was not quite sure what they thought the alternative would have been. Considering that before the show they sent a chauffeur-driven and luxurious limousine with coffee and sweets but as soon as the show was over they wanted to know if I preferred to walk or have a cab, I figured I had become a has-been rather quickly. Andy Warhol said everybody gets fifteen minutes of fame and my limo ride had lasted thirty minutes, so I guess I had no right to complain.

According to the syndication schedule the producer gave me, the show was going to air on the following Friday at 9 a.m. in New York, my hometown. There wasn't time to write notes to people to watch the show so I made about twenty phone calls, some to people that had never before seen 9 a.m. I must confess I was pretty excited about being on national television.

Friday morning I awoke at 5 a.m., and waited to call New York until 6 a.m. California time (9 a.m. in New York) to see how I looked on national television. At exactly 6:05, I called my ex-wife in New York and excitedly asked her how I looked. She had kept our three children home from school to watch their father on national TV. My ex-wife said, "There is some dentist on with several children discussing what the sugar in candy and cake does to their teeth." Frustrated, I screamed at her, "You have the wrong channel on." She told me it could not be the wrong channel because it was the *Phil Donahue Show*. I panicked and immediately called Chicago only to get no answer. It then dawned on me that it was only slightly after 8 o'clock in Chicago with the two-hour time difference between California and Chicago.

Finally, after a grueling hour wait, I reached somebody at the *Donahue Show* who informed me that they thought the taping was too good to air in September and deserved to be seen by the larger October viewing audience. They had decided to put the show on hold and air it in four weeks.

What was I going to tell those bleary-eyed people who had lost a good night's sleep on my behalf? I felt so embarrassed, I didn't have the nerve to call back the people who had gotten up at 9 a.m. to watch me only to find some children discussing cavities! I never informed them of the new air date.

After the show aired in October, I was contacted by the *David Susskind Show* in New York, and *60 Minutes* to appear on their shows on the same issue. It was at this point that I decided that while I was having fun traveling around the country doing these shows, I was taking a lot of time away from my business, and needed to figure out a way to make some money out of it. My ego had been totally indulged by seeing myself on the "national tube" and it was now time to turn the situation into some financial remuneration.

It dawned on me to write a book on the subject so that when I did these shows I could at least plug my book. In addition, and more importantly, the Lee Marvin trial was approximately one year off and I was sure it would provide a million dollars worth of free publicity for a book on the subject.

Encouraged by the fact that everybody seemed to like my writing when it came to the *Ingleside Bedtime Stories*, plus the fact that everything I touched or tried to accomplish since I had come to Palm Springs had been successful, I felt I was on a roll and that my next conquest would be that of becoming a best-selling author.

Actually, I do not write — I dictate, as if I am telling someone a story, and if my writing is enjoyable, it is for the reason that I am a reasonably good storyteller, but not necessarily a good writer. I remember that in my prior business career people would often comment that my letters seemed as if I were talking to the reader. I always explained that, in fact, it was because I dictated the letter as though they were sitting in front of me and I was talking to them.

The point of my book was going to be that you did not have to be a movie star, like Lee Marvin, or a celebrity to be involved in a palimony law suit. I intended to take a serious look at the issue, tell a little bit of my story, which I felt contained some interesting elements and, at the same time, have my sense of humor surface throughout the book. This was taking place during the fall of 1979, when I had begun to undertake to build a glamorous supper club/discotheque combination in Palm Springs by the name of Cecil's.

In those days, I was loaded with boundless energy and my daily pattern consisted of: getting up at 4 a.m.; dictating several pages of the palimony book; dropping them off at a secretarial service by 7 a.m.; spending the day at Cecil's trying to get it organized and built; on returning home in the evening at approximately 6 p.m., picking up the typed pages that the secretarial service finished that day; and, editing those before I went to sleep only to get up at 4 a.m. the following morning and dictate more pages.

I was actually quite proud of the book after the final edit was finished. I thought I had accomplished everything I had set out to do and was particularly proud of the title I had chosen, considering the topic of the book. The title of the book was, *I Take This Man — For Everything He's Got*, subtitled, *The Case Against Palimony*. I had even taken a picture with my current girlfriend which I felt would be perfect as the cover illustration. It depicted a man and a woman in a very passionate embrace and, while her arms are around him, hugging him, she is slipping his wallet out of his back pocket.

While it was not the "Great American Novel" that most people fantasize about writing, I knew it would be a commercial success. I felt totally confident that my literary career would be launched by this book.

Now that I had manuscript in-hand, I had no idea what to do next. In speaking to several of my knowledgeable customers at Melvyn's, it became apparent that the next step was to engage a literary agent. One of my customers recommended one in New York whom I immediately contacted. He requested a copy of the manuscript which I promptly sent to him via Federal Express. The agent called up approximately three days later, very excited, and said he felt it had great commercial potential. I explained to him that I didn't write books for a living and did not necessarily need any advance money, but felt it would make interesting reading considering the controversial and timely nature of the subject.

I had previously arranged to go to New York in April to appear on the *David Susskind Show,* as well as to attend a family celebration. I asked the agent to line up appointments with three of the top publishing houses in New York for the week that I would be there, so he and I could visit them. This would be ideal since I would be appearing on the *Susskind Show* to discuss the palimony issue on the following Sunday. I gave him my schedule and two weeks later the agent confirmed our appointments with three top publishing houses.

Now that I was an accomplished author represented by a professional agent, my main concern was where I should hold the first book-signing party. This kept me totally occupied on the flight to New York. Already I was mentally thinking of my next book. As soon as I checked into my hotel in New York the phone rang. It was my agent. Obviously he knew he had a great author on his hands and was anxious to get started! I told him I needed just a few minutes to freshen up and would meet him downstairs in the bar.

Upon entering the bar of the hotel, I was shown to a corner booth by the Maitre d.' As I approached the booth, I thought there had to be some mistake since the gentleman sitting there had hair that almost reached down to his waist, an earring in one ear and was wearing a t-shirt, blue jeans and slippers. He appeared to be in his early thirties. He stood up, extended his hand and introduced himself. As soon as the shock wore off, I reasoned to myself that the literary world was full of intellectuals with very individual ideas and non-conformists who indulged themselves in total freedom of expression. Over a cocktail, my agent discussed the three appointments he had set up with the various major publishing houses as well as his background of success in getting books published. I felt very confident that I had made the right choice…in spite of his appearance.

The following morning at 9 a.m. we showed up at our first appointment. We were escorted into the office of the vice-president of this particular publishing house. I quickly went into my pitch: the fact that I didn't write books for a living but felt that the Lee Marvin trial, which was now seven months away, would sell the book. I was feeling pretty cocky and I explained that I did not need any advance money for the book. However, since the Lee Marvin decision was a "first," I felt I had good story to tell and needed a publisher mainly for the distribution. I went so far as to say that if they didn't want to pay for the publishing of the book, I was so confident of its success that I would actually pay for it. But, based on the fact that I was taking the entire financial gamble, I said that I would expect some additional compensation instead of just receiving the usual royalties. I then explained that I would be appearing on *David Susskind* that coming Sunday night, and he could tune in if he had any doubts as to whether or not I could sell the book. As part of the deal, I offered to do as many television or radio shows as they could arrange in thirty days in order to promote the book once it was in the stores.

My presentation took approximately fifteen minutes and during this entire time I was getting no reaction from the vice-president. The agent sat quietly by, watching me sell. The more I talked, the more enthusiastic I got, and the faster I talked. When I had said everything

I could think of, the vice president simply replied that he would let us know as soon as a decision was reached. He thanked us for considering his company to publish the book. And with that, we left.

I walked out of there not knowing whether I had made my point or not. I felt totally frustrated because, based on my past experience in judging people, I usually had a pretty good idea whether I left an impression or not.

The following two meetings were almost identical with the first. The agent did his best to assure me that these were not emotional people, that publishers were basically very conservative but he felt sure that at least one of them would come back with an offer. He told me not to expect to hear anything for at least two weeks. I had done my best to impress each one that time was of the essence, that the impetus for sales would be the Lee Marvin trial, and that it was important that the book be on the stands when the trial took place.

That following Sunday I appeared on the *David Susskind Show* and, at the risk of sounding conceited, I thought it was a great show. The panel consisted of me, Marvin Mitchelson (the lawyer suing Lee Marvin), the head of the Chicago Matrimonial Trial Lawyers Association, and the head of the New York Matrimonial Trial Lawyers Association. Three accomplished lawyers and little old me. I must tell you I did a lot better than just hold my own.

I returned to Palm Springs and two weeks later my agent called to say that all three publishing houses had turned us down. I was shocked and could not believe it — I was so certain that it would have been a commercial success. When you fail at something, you search for the reasons why, and the best one I could come up with was — you hire an agent to sell you...you don't try to sell yourself. I guess I came off as being conceited, arrogant and cocky.

I was totally disillusioned with the literary business. I envisioned that when you wrote a book you became the darling of the intellectual set, the guest of honor at many cocktail parties and immediately received national recognition for your wit and intellect. As far as I was concerned, based on my experience, it was no different than selling storm screens, windows, or vacuum cleaners. It was a business like everything else. I was still aggravated over having failed at getting my book published, especially because of all the time and energy I put into it, plus the fact that I hated to miss the recognition and dollars I knew the book would generate.

I was circulating in my restaurant on a busy Saturday saying hello to several familiar faces when all of a sudden a bell went off in my head and I doubled back to some people I had just greeted. I remembered that one of them, a young man named Ira, had something to do with publishing. I went back to his table and said, "If you don't mind me asking, Ira, don't you have something to do with publishing?" He said, "Yes, I just bought *Playgirl Magazine* and we have turned it around and are doing quite well with it." Without worrying about being rude by interrupting his dinner with his three guests, I immediately launched into the sorrowful tale of my lost literary career. Ira suggested I give him a copy of the manuscript. He said he would be happy to read it and give me his personal opinion. I rushed up to my office to make sure that Ira left that night with my book in his hand and made him promise to get back to me as soon as he had digested it.

Three days later, Ira called and said he was very excited about the book, loved it, and not only would he get it published but he would even serialize it in *Playgirl Magazine*. He asked me when I could come up to his offices in Santa Monica, California, and I asked him if the next day would be too soon. The next day, Ira showed me around his new impressive offices, introduced me to key members of his staff, and then we sat down at his conference table.

He told his secretary to get so-and-so in New York on the phone. The secretary buzzed him and said she had the party on the line. After a brief greeting, Ira told someone on the other end that he had this book he wanted published and that he would serialize it. He introduced me over the phone to this publisher in New York who told me that as soon as I could hire a literary attorney to represent me, he would have the contracts drawn, we would both sign, and we would be in business. My faith in humanity had been restored, although in my heart I had known I was on the right track all along. I immediately hired a literary attorney recommended by Ira and he negotiated a contract with the publishers in New York on my behalf. There were no advance fees involved so it was a reasonably easy deal to draw. As I sent my copy of the manuscript off to New York I tried to impress upon them that time was of the essence since the Lee Marvin trial was now only five months away. After two weeks passed, I called the publishers in New York to ask them how we were doing, and they told me that they had the perfect rewrite person in mind for my book but she was in the process of finishing another project. Another two weeks went by, I called, and was told the same story again. Three more weeks passed and I was beginning to get very nervous about the timing of the project. I was no dummy — I knew exactly how to push them! I sent a telegram, "Please publish immediately or return manuscript at once." The manuscript came back so fast it almost knocked my head off. So much for wise guy!

The Lee Marvin trial caused national headlines for over 30 days, as I imagined, and I was sick over the missed opportunity. The next few months I received inquiries about my book from various people who indicated they might be interested in representing me or trying to get the book published. At this point, I had lost all interest, since the issue was no longer timely and the main thrust for the sale of the book, the Lee Marvin trial, was over.

As a result of this experience I completely lost my desire to be a writer and could no longer bring myself to write at all. (I don't know if this is indicative of my lack of tenacity and perseverance in the face of adversity.) In spite of the fact that as the years passed many of our hotel guests who had read the original edition of the *Ingleside Inn Bedtime Stories* requested that I write more, I could not get up the creative energy to do so.

However, in December of 1988, a guest of the hotel absolutely astounded me by showing up at the hotel one Saturday morning and showed me a professionally published copy of *Ingleside Inn Bedtime Stories*. I was totally astonished and asked him what it was all about and he said, "I thought you might enjoy this as a present. There are 500 of these in my car and I would appreciate it if you would help me unload them." I was dumfounded and didn't know how to respond or what to say.

After bringing the cartons in, I meekly asked, "How much would this have cost me if I had ordered them?" He replied, "About $6,000." I was so overwhelmed I said to him, "I don't know what to do with these." I was in a state of shock. He suggested, "Why don't you sell them for charity?" Fortunately, I am the president of a very worthwhile local charity.

Excited, I ran down to the restaurant and told the story to several customers whom I knew quite well. They asked how much I was going to charge for the book and, although I had $10 in mind, I asked them what they thought. One of the customers said, "I think you should autograph them and sell them for $25 a copy." I replied, "OK." He promptly pulled $100 out of his pocket, bought four books, took one to another table, told them the story, and they bought four! I could not believe it but I had raised $200 in ten minutes!

Our local newspaper, the *Desert Sun*, heard about it and sent a reporter to interview me. They did a major story on my book and how it came to be professionally published. They very cleverly titled the article, "Tales He Could Tell." As a result of the article, the sales of the book were rather brisk and several thousand dollars were raised pretty quickly for the Angel View Crippled Children's Foundation.

The following month I was invited to be a guest speaker before the Palm Springs Writers Guild. Having found out that the previous speaker had been Elliott Roosevelt, our former president's son, I was quite honored to be invited. I received quite a nice reception and was invited to speak to various different organizations. I was truly basking in the light focused on my intellect and wit.

You never know what it takes to inspire you. It was the gift of those 500 books that has motivated me to attempt to write again, if for no other reason than to relieve the boredom of the Ingleside Inn regulars who have been reading the same bedtime stories over and over again.

Should my literary career ever truly succeed, I owe it all to Mr. Carl Bennitt.

THE CAR CONNOISSEUR

As a result of acquiring a reputation as a car collector, I started to fancy myself as one. For my 36th birthday, back in New York, I had bought myself a Rolls Royce. I had more than my share of problems with it. On one hand it was a great thrill to own a Rolls but on the other hand, due to the scarcity of people who are qualified to fix them, and the expense involved, it was really a headache.

However, I must admit, there is a prestige about a Rolls unequalled by any other luxury item I know. It never ceased to amaze me, the attention and importance one received when driving a Rolls.

The coup de grace was one time in New York. I was visiting a friend at his boat in a Long Island marina. He greeted me in the parking lot with an acquaintance. His friend really seemed quite impressed and looked jealously at the car, like a child looking in a toy store window. I later discovered this gentleman owned a $200,000 boat that I was very impressed with. (He could have owned six Rolls Royces for the price of this boat!) I guess the point to that is, different strokes for different folks.

When I first came to California, I had a hang-loose attitude, so I left my Rolls for sale in New York. When I hit California, I bought a 3-year-old Fiat. It was perfect for my new identity. It suited cut-off jeans, sneakers with no socks and a tee shirt. Talk about hanging loose! Going from a Rolls Royce to a used Fiat was like going from a steam bath into an ice cold pool. I felt like I was drifting in space. For the moment, showy things were no longer important. Little did I know that this was only a temporary phase in my life.

I was in California about three months when I recognized the necessity of getting my live-in girlfriend a car. That weekend we were heading for Palm Springs to stay at a friend's house. He had informed me that I would be sharing it with another couple, a business associate and his wife. They were nice enough and all four of us got along great. Saturday night we were all sitting around the kitchen table and my friend's business associate was looking through the auto section of the Sunday paper, checking on his ad to sell his Mercedes. I asked him about the car and he described it and gave me the model number. Mercedes model numbers have always been too complicated for my small brain. I often wondered why they didn't use model names like the American manufacturers do. But, I was pretty sure I knew which model he was talking about and I agreed to buy the car.

Later that evening my lady and I went out for drinks and by coincidence we ran into the Palm Springs Mercedes dealer. I described the model and the deal to him, and he said that the four-seater Mercedes convertible was a good investment and he offered me $1,000 more than I was paying. I never ever look a gift horse in the mouth and, satisfied that I was making a hell of a buy, I rushed back to the house. I played it very casual not wanting to alert the seller that I was stealing his car. I made like it was not a big deal and because I trusted him to give me a fair shake I would buy it sight unseen. I gave him a check in full for the car and made an appointment to pick it up Monday in Los Angeles. He was thrilled.

Monday morning at the appointed time in L.A., we met at a gas station. He was standing on the corner. I pulled up and asked him where the car was. He pointed toward the gas station where there were six or seven cars. Not seeing a convertible four-seater Mercedes, "I asked — which one?" He said, "Right there. The little two-seater!" I couldn't believe it. I was sure I was buying a convertible four-seater Mercedes which was worth $5,000 more than the two-seater convertible. Because of our previous conversation, I was too embarrassed to tell the seller that his car was a different model than the one I thought I was buying. I quickly figured out that instead of paying under wholesale, I had paid top retail — another credit to my astute abilities as a horse trader.

About two months later, while staying at this same friend's house in Palm Springs, I noticed his next door neighbor drive up one day in a very unique looking car. When I asked about the car, the neighbor informed me that it was a Bugatti replica. I fell in love with the car. It was classier than a dune buggy but not quite a real automobile. It was a two-seater, racing car-style, built on a Volkswagen chassis

144

and seemed perfect to use in the desert as a toy. I asked the neighbor if he was interested in selling the car and he said, "Absolutely." I asked how much he wanted and he replied, "Four thousand." I agreed to purchase the car.

I wrote him my personal check and asked him for a copy of the pink slip, deeding the ownership over to me. He told me it was in a safety deposit box at the bank and could not get to it until Monday (this was Saturday). However, he did agree to give me possession of the car immediately, as long as I turned my check over to him.

I was very excited. I got my girlfriend to take a ride with me. I drove around for about forty minutes to many admiring glances and whistles. I stopped at a traffic light, whereupon the guy in the car next to me asked me where I got the car. I proudly told him I had just bought it and wasn't it great? He asked me if I could pull over for a second as he'd like to speak with me.

We both pulled over at the next corner and he asked me again where I got the car. I told him the name of the guy I bought the car from, and how much I paid for it. He asked if I had the pink slip and I explained I would not have it until Monday. He said, "You will never have the pink slip because I own this car. I loaned it to that man to display at a charity golf tournament."

I could not believe my ears because the gentleman I purchased the car from was a prominent realtor in Palm Springs, very well-known and although I had come from Brooklyn and heard the story about people buying the Brooklyn Bridge, it had never happened to me before. I immediately rushed back to my friend's house and called the neighbor. He said he was busy and couldn't see me right then. I said, "You'd better come out and see me right now or the police will be at your door." He came over immediately and asked me what the problem was. I explained to him that the real owner of the car had just pulled me over and told me that I had bought the car from somebody who didn't own it. The neighbor replied that he had every intention of buying the car from the owner on Monday and then selling it to me.

Needless to say, I got my check back and called him every name in the book. Today he is still a very prominent person in Palm Springs and avoids me everytime we bump into each other. I wonder why?

I was still intrigued with the Bugatti replica and looked up the man who really owned the car. He ran a body and fender shop in town and had built the car himself on a Volkswagen chassis. He told me he knew where there were several of the fiberglass replica kits and if I was interested he would build the cars for me. I figured this would be a perfect sideline venture to get into. The main purpose, of course, would be to acquire one for myself.

I bought the five available fiberglass kits, had them shipped to the body and fender shop, and registered a company name, "The Great American Automobile Company." (Watch out, Ford, Chrysler and General Motors!) Bob, the body and fender man, had given me a price of $1,500 each to assemble the cars and I figured that all the components, including the kit, would cost another $1,500 for a total of $3,000 each. My idea was to sell four of them for $5,000 each. That would give me a $5,000 profit and one free Bugatti for myself. I used Bob's car as the sales model and kept it parked in front of the Ingleside Inn. The amount of interest and curiosity it generated was absolutely incredible.

My first sale was to Xavier Cugat, the famous Latin bandleader, who ordered it as a surprise birthday present for his then wife, Charo. He ordered it to be painted bright fire engine red and told me that when it was ready I should call him so he could stage a party around its delivery. Approximately sixty days later, I called Mr. Cugat and we arranged for me to deliver the car the following Thursday at 6 p.m. to his home in Beverly Hills. At the appointed time, I hid the car around the corner, rang the doorbell and was instructed to drive the car into their rather large courtyard. When I drove the car through the gates, I noticed Charo was blindfolded and as I parked the car, the blindfold was removed and she shrieked with delight. Charo was absolutely thrilled with the present and immediately jumped in to take the car for a drive. There was one minor problem. Charo did not know how to drive a stick shift.

I was invited to stay for dinner, which I did. During the evening, Mr. Cugat graciously offered to do an original painting of all the celebrities that had come into my restaurant, Melvyn's, as a token of his appreciation. I was extremely pleased by an offer of this magnitude from such a renown artist. (He did, in fact, do the painting which characterizes some sixty different celebrities. In fact, the original was reproduced and sold as a lithograph in various art galleries. The original oil is hanging in my home.)

The month after I had delivered the car to Charo, *New West Magazine* did a feature story on her and in several of the pictures she posed in her new red Bugatti. *Esquire Magazine* contacted me about the car and actually ran a small article about it with a picture of the Bugatti replica, and listed the manufacturer as the Great American Automobile Company of Palm Springs. I was really beginning to enjoy this.

One day, George Hamilton, the actor, and his friend, Jimmy Randall, came to dinner at Melvyn's. They called me over to their table to inquire about the Bugatti that was sitting in the driveway. I explained that it was a replica, built on a Volkswagen chassis and that it cost $5,000. Jimmy Randall pulled out his checkbook, wrote me a check for $10,000 and asked me to have one delivered to him and one to George Hamilton in L.A. This was certainly beginning to turn into something fun. That left only two Bugattis and I wanted to keep one for myself, just to run around in, so that left one to sell.

One morning at about 11 a.m., I was sitting in my office when the front desk informed me there was a Mr. Pepper to see me. I was warned that he was pretty shabby-looking. As I went out to the front desk I was faced with somebody that can best be described as looking like a homeless person. His clothes were filthy. He had a long straggly beard, needed a haircut, wore no socks and his sneakers looked like they would disintegrate at any moment. He appeared to be about 32 years old and, in my opinion, was either stoned or drunk. Mr. Pepper said he wanted some information about the Bugatti sitting in the driveway. Not wanting to waste my time, I simply said, "It's $6,000 and if you have any interest, please call me." I gave him one of my business cards and he left.

About twenty minutes later, I was called by my front office again. Mr. Pepper was back. Really annoyed this time, I approached with the sole purpose of brushing him off nicely. As I came to the front desk, Mr. Pepper handed me an envelope and said, "You'll find $6,000 cash inside. Please give me the pink slip and the keys." Whoever said, "You can't judge a book by its cover," must have had Mr. Pepper in mind!

After about six months in California, I decided to have my Rolls Royce shipped from New York, since I couldn't find a buyer there. When the trucking company delivered the car, instead of feeling elation, I felt like my headache had followed me from New York. The Rolls sitting in front of my restaurant alongside the attention-getting Bugatti, enhanced my reputation as an auto enthusiast. I noticed that whenever a newspaper or magazine would write something on the Inn or Restaurant, they always mentioned the cars.

Just about that time, a friend of mine from New York called because he heard I was collecting cars. He described a one-only custom-built Rolls Royce limousine that was built for and owned by a Lord in England. It had just been shipped to New York and was available at a very reasonable price. I knew the Rolls Royce market was getting hot, plus I rationalized it would be great to use as the hotel's limousine. I bought it over the phone.

The limo was shipped cross-country by truck and I made sure the local newspaper was in attendance at its arrival. It was a very impressive-looking automobile. It had a divider window and a spin-around bar in the back. A picture of me and the car appeared in the newspaper the following day. As I was showing the article to a customer in the restaurant, he commented that publicity like that was good for getting robbed. That night my condominium was burglarized. They took everything, including my clothes. As I am writing this, it has just dawned on me for the first time, that maybe it was my friend who made that comment who robbed me.

The Rolls limo was a very impressive sight sitting in front of the restaurant, and enhanced my reputation as a car collector. By this time, I was beginning to enjoy the reputation and because of it, some very interesting and substantial people were introducing themselves to me. They were serious collectors and, at the beginning, I made jokes about my reputation but discovered very quickly it was not the thing to do.

One day, Colonel Russell Hopf, of 'Sir John fame' (Chapter Two), called and said he would like to see me. I hadn't seen the Colonel since Sir John's arrest. He told me that he still had the two Rolls Royces that he had originally tried to sell Sir John and needed to liquidate them as his partner was in a cash bind. One was a 1947 Sedanca once owned by Sir Lawrence Olivier, and the other was a 1934 Rolls touring car in which Babs Hutton's first husband, Prince Midavani, was killed. It had been her wedding present to him and the car had quite a history. I bought the two cars as an investment.

Now, I kept my four Rolls Royces (the limo, the two I just bought and my personal car) parked in front of the restaurant and, boy, were the customers impressed. I must admit I was too. I established high prices in my own mind for each car so that, even if I didn't sell them, at least the figures would dazzle the public.

One day, a guy at the bar introduced himself to me. He said he was from Florida and was interested in purchasing one of the cars to use in California where he spent a great deal of time on business. I quickly rattled off the prices, while pointing each one out through the restaurant window. Very nonchalantly he said he would take the beige Silver Shadow which was my original car from New York and the one I was most anxious to sell. He told me to get the registration slip and he would make out a check for it.

There were two things I was never able to keep organized: keys and car registrations. With two Bugattis, a Fiat, four Rolls Royces, a Mercedes, two Cadillac limousines, and several others, I owned a total of thirteen cars. I searched frantically through my files for the registration but could not find it. After twenty minutes, I got nervous and went back to the man at the bar and suggested we finish the transaction the following day so I could thoroughly search for the registration. He explained that he was going back to Florida that evening but he would leave a draft for the money at his bank at Newport Beach. All I would have to do is present the registration at the bank and they would turn over the funds. I agreed to let him take the car so he could have it put into tip-top shape at the Rolls Royce dealer in Newport.

I searched through all my files to no avail. I couldn't locate the registration. I called his bank in Newport on Monday morning and explained the situation. I suggested that I would give the buyer a bill of sale and that he should apply for a new registration. The banker informed me that his instructions were to only turn over the funds if a clear title was presented. The buyer was out of the country and I couldn't reach him. I was very frustrated as I had been trying to sell that particular car for over a year and half. Finally, after going through every paper in my files four times, I found the registration. I was overjoyed. I ran down to my bank, so they could present it to the buyer's bank for the draft.

Two days later, the buyer's banker called. The first thing he said was, "What are you trying to pull?" I was startled and asked him what he was referring to. He told me the registration I sent belonged to a Volkswagon. I didn't own a Volkswagen. Furthermore he had called the Department of Motor Vehicles in Sacramento and there was no such car as 539NCR (my license plate number) in their files. I got angry and said, "Number one, I am not trying to pull anything. Number two, I own that car. And, Number three, I didn't manufacture those license plates in my bedroom. They were issued to me by the DMV in Palm Springs." I told him I would call him back.

I was really infuriated. By being so anxious to close the deal, it looked like I was trying to pull a swindle. It suddenly dawned on me that the Volkswagen registration was for one of the five Bugatti's which were built on a VW chassis. I immediately called the DMV in Sacramento and explained my problem. I told them my license plate was 539NCR and could they please check who the owner was. By this time it was about 4 o'clock in the afternoon and they told me if they didn't get back to me the next day, it would be the day after.

The following day in the mail I received my bill of sale back from the bank in Newport, with a note stating the buyer no longer wanted to purchase the car and I should make arrangements to have it picked up in Newport Beach within two days. I still hadn't heard from the DMV so I called them back. The women I had spoken to informed me that there was no such license plate as 539NCR. I was ready to pull my hair out. When I had the car shipped out from New York I had gone down to the DMV in Palm Springs, registered it and they issued me California plates 539NCR.

The whole situation was absolutely ridiculous but a typical Mel Haber situation. I went through every piece of paper in my office and finally came up with a suspense receipt which they issued to me when I got the plates. I called back the DMV with this information and after two days more they finally discovered that they had never issued the registration or put the information in the computer because they didn't have my address. It seemed to me like that car and I were destined to be together for life.

Unwilling to accept that I was going to have a companion for life that I didn't want, I began to actively pursue selling the car. Over the four years I had owned the automobile, I probably had spent more than $10,000 repairing it. It was again in need of some major work. I made a consignment deal with a mechanic in San Diego whereby he would do $2,000 worth of work and only get paid when he sold the car. I gave him a price to sell the car at $2,000 under the market and was happy just to get the car out of my sight. In the meantime, I told everybody I came in contact with that I wanted to sell the car.

I was in L.A. when a local and well-known 'flake' called me at my hotel. He had a small car rental business and asked me if I would be interested in leasing the Rolls I was trying to sell. He told me he had a customer who wanted to lease a Rolls and was very interested in mine.

He told me he checked the guy out and his credit was good. The customer was going to put $3,000 down and his first four year's payments would equal what I was asking for the car. If the customer decided then to purchase the car he would have to pay an additional $12,000. This meant over four years I would receive what I was asking for the car plus I would still own the car. What a deal! I was excited. Finally I was going to make out.

The "flake" told me he wanted a $2,000 commission and he would handle the whole transaction. I figured with a $3,000 down-payment and still owning the car, there was no way I could go wrong. He explained the customer had to have the car the following day as he was leaving on a trip and if I could get the car back from the mechanic in San Diego, he would handle everything. I was not able to cut my L.A. trip short so I called the mechanic in San Diego and told him to deliver the car to Palm Springs to the hotel and they would give him $2,000 for the work he had done.

I called my bookkeeper and instructed him to give the mechanic $2,000 and the car leasing guy $2,000 upon presentation of a car lease with a $3,000 check. This was on a Thursday and when I returned on Monday at 11 a.m., the transaction had just been completed two hours before. I was thrilled.

That evening, the car rental guy called and told me the customer had almost gotten to L.A.(110 miles) before the car broke down. He found a mechanic and had the car towed into L.A. I had just paid $2,000 to the mechanic in San Diego to put the car in tip-top shape—everything should have proceeded without a hitch, but that would have been too easy!

The man who leased the car called me and asked me to wire money to the mechanic in L.A. I told him I was sorry but I had just paid a guy in San Diego to fix it, and I was not about to pay a guy in Beverly Hills for the same thing. The man was so excited about his first Rolls Royce that he said he would pay the bill himself. Four days passed and the bank called and told me his check bounced. I couldn't believe it. I was now out $3,000 plus my car. The car rental guy and I both tried frantically to reach the customer only to find that he was driving the car cross-country to Baltimore. Frankly, I would have been scared to drive that car four blocks!

The next morning I received a call from the mechanic in Beverly Hills who asked what address I wanted the bill sent to. "What bill?" I screamed. He explained a guy came in with a brown Rolls that needed work and told him that it was owned by Mel Haber and would be paid for by Mel Haber. The mechanic had heard of my reputation as a Rolls collector and did the work based on that. He didn't want to hear any stories. I owned the car, he did the work on it and he wanted his $541. I told him I would get back to him. I had often joked with people by saying, "Don't worry, things will get worse before they get better." But this was ridiculous. This brown Rolls seemed to be my personal cross to bear and I was beginning to sag under its weight.

During the next four days the mechanic had called five times, finally threatening to sue me. Two and a half weeks after I leased the car, I got another call from the guy who rented it. It seems he was in Chicago with not one, but two blowouts and wanted to know what was I going to do about it. I fought to keep my composure lest he abandon the car. I told him that his check had bounced and the mechanic he said he was going to pay was trying to sue me. He said he would handle all that when he got back in three weeks but what was I going to do about the tires. I told him he could deduct two new tires from his first payment and when he came back we would sit down and resolve everything.

He pointed out that he wasn't spending that kind of money for all this aggravation. I told him at this point, it was I, not he, who was spending money; that I had as much aggravation, if not more, and had no car and no money. After 1½ hours, we both calmed down and decided to wait until he got back.

The following day I received a summons from Small Claims Court from the mechanic in Beverly Hills. By this time I was screaming at the car leasing guy. I wanted my $2,000 commission back. He was a "bust-out" type guy and was offering to pay me back $100 a month. I was expecting a fatal heart attack any minute and didn't think I would live the 20 months to get paid back. Four more days passed and my heart was almost beating regularly again when I received a call from the Atlanta police. My car had been impounded after being involved in a major accident. There was major damage done to the car and it was undrivable. The driver was in jail on a bad check charge.

I arranged for a repossession company to pick up the car and ship it back to Palm Springs. The Atlanta police were nice enough to send me pictures and it looked like about $3,000 damage. One of the clauses in the lease was that the lessee was supposed to provide me proof of insurance which he had done. However, three days before this point, I had received notice of cancellation from his insurance company due to non-payment of the premium.

Two weeks later the car had its second trip to Palm Springs by truck. The first time it came as my headache. The second time it came as 'my coronary.' Needless to say, the car had fallen off the truck during the trip back but at this point that was anticlimactic. After paying the mechanic, trucking, and repossession companies and computing all the costs involved, I figured the deal cost me about $9,000. I sold the car in an "as-is" condition to a body shop in Los Angeles. The owner kept the car for himself. I ran into him recently and he thanked me profusely. He said it was the best car he ever owned.

Having a reputation as a car collector, as I said previously, brings one in contact with many interesting people. It is like an ailment you get that you've never heard of. All of a sudden everybody has either had it or knows somebody who has it. Everybody had a deal for me. There were several guys in L.A. making a living brokering deals on cars. I was high on their prospect list because I had a reputation for buying cars 'sight unseen' over the telephone. This was due to my trust in my fellow man. I don't remember ever hearing the famous words, "Buyer Beware."

One day a guy called me from L.A. to sell me a 15-year-old Mercedes car. Surprised that I didn't know the model and confused that I didn't just send him a check, he decided to have the car sent to me on a consignment basis for a week. It was about this time that I was becoming disillusioned with my hobby.

Due to the fact that I bought cars without having them checked out, plus the fact that I bought based on price primarily, my collection always had a high percentage of bad cars. At the peak of my car career, I figured at any given moment 65-70% of my cars were at various mechanics for repairs.

A Mercedes convertible dealer from L.A. stayed at my hotel for a week and I tried desperately to make a deal with him to trade off some of my "dogs." I had always found it easy to buy but somewhat more difficult to sell. This guy was too smart for me and I decided to return his car to him. I had to have some special work done on my Rolls limo in L.A. so I arranged with my son and his friend to drive both the Mercedes convertible and the Rolls Royce limo into L.A. Coincidentally, the dealer in L.A. had a car that had to come back to Palm Springs so it was going to work out perfectly.

Now I must tell you about my son Lonny. He was 18-years old then, good looking, well-built, heart of gold, nice boy — but one of those people who constantly walks around with a little cloud over their head. If something can possibly go wrong, it always does with Lonny.

Lonny and his friend left early in the morning to deliver the two cars to L.A. They had been gone about three hours and Lonny called. I knew immediately something was wrong. "Dad, we had a little accident," he said. Not really wanting to know, I asked, "What happened?" It seems that when they were exiting the freeway, Lonny's friend, who was driving the Mercedes, slowed down on the off ramp. Lonny was following in the Rolls limo and was looking the other way and rear-ended the Mercedes with the Rolls limo; not just damage to one car, but to both—at the same time.

During the height of my 'car-collecting career' I always had several of my cars in the driveway of the Ingleside Inn. I frequently joked that a decent accident could wipe out at least two of my cars at one time. Well now it finally happened. Knowing Lonny, I told him not to worry, but to make sure he drove back carefully with the dealer's car. When I hung up I said to myself, "If this is all that happens, I will be getting away lucky."

About an hour later I received a call from the Beverly Hills Police Department. They just arrested two young boys driving a Rolls limo the wrong way on a one-way street. Neither one had a license or the car registration and both said they worked for me. Fortunately, I was able to convince the policemen to let them go. I felt like hiding somewhere until they got home. Five more hours passed and I knew something had happened. Finally there was a knock at my front door. It was Lonny. His first words were, "Dad, you won't believe what happened!" It seemed to be his standard greeting.

I looked out past him at his friend standing in the driveway next to a car that I would describe as totally demolished. Both doors were smashed in, the windows broken, and the front grill was practically in the front seat — a definite loser in a demolition derby.

I was afraid to have them come in to tell the story for fear my house would collapse. We stood in the driveway as Lonny described the first accident of their return trip. That wasn't too bad because they had only sideswiped another car on the freeway. The second accident was a real beauty. In order to avoid a car that had stopped suddenly in front of them, the friend had steered the car into the center divider, bouncing off and hitting a truck. The car we were all leaning on had been a brand new Datsun only three short hours before. The whole thing was too outrageous to even be upset about.

The whole situation was really very simple to resolve. All I had to do was fix the Rolls limo, fix the Mercedes convertible, send the Beverly Hills police copies of my son and his friend's licenses and the Rolls limo's registration, pay the tickets, fix the first car my son and his friend sideswiped, fix the truck they bounced into, pay the State of California for the broken divider, and replace the brand-new Datsun. No big deal!! It could have been worse but I'm not sure how.

I think everything that could possibly happen happened during my car collecting period—

I sold my personal Rolls Royce to a car leasing company in California and now, six months later, have not been paid because of a complication with the New York Motor Vehicle Bureau where the car was originally registered.

I sold another Rolls through one of the country's foremost car auction companies and am now suing to get the money because they were held up for the receipts at the end of the auction. I am not quite sure what that has to do with me.

I bought an old Daimler and gave it to a shop in L.A. for total restoration. Now, 2½ years later, I have yet to see the car.

Having acquired a reputation as a well-known car collector, I was approached on a constant basis by various people connected with the automotive business. When the custom-built Clinet automobile was first offered, one was offered to me at an inside price of $30,000. Within two years, they were selling, used, for $50,000. I felt like kicking myself.

About that same time, the legendary Hollywood car-customizer, George Barris, (who built the Batmobile and other special Hollywood cars) approached me about buying a custom car he was building to be called, the Barrister, to be built on a Corvette chassis. He was going to start off by building only ten. He already had several orders from movie stars such as Bo Derrick, James Caan, Sammy Davis, etc. but felt the exposure I could give the car in Palm Springs would be great for him. He showed me a prototype of the car and I fell in love with it. George wanted $50,000 for the car (and I had visions of it doubling in price rather quickly, especially considering he was making a very limited edition). I called up George and told him that I would buy a car under one condition, I wanted the first one, Number One, for the publicity as well as the investment value. Mr. Barris said that was impossible because Bo Derrick was getting Number One, James Caan was getting Number Two, Sammy Davis was getting Number Three, and on and on and on. I told him the only way I would buy the car was if I got Number One…and he went through the same routine all over again.

I really wanted the car and came up with an absolutely brilliant scheme. Bo Derrick's movie *"10"* had just come out and was a big success. I called back George Barris and said, "George, call up Bo Derrick and tell her she should have Number Ten, and if she goes for it, give me Number One, and you've made a sale." George thought it was a great idea.

George called me back one hour later and said we had a deal — that I would get Number One. I must tell you I was really excited and I immediately sent him a deposit on the car. George promised me delivery within 90 days. I asked him to send me paint and upholstery color samples for me to choose from. George insisted that I leave it up to him — that it would be spectacular.

I was so excited and anxious to see the car that I called the factory every week just to find out about the progress of my car. I told anybody and everybody about it who would listen to me. Finally, after approximately four months, George announced that he would be delivering the car during an auto show in Palm Springs the following week. I could hardly contain myself.

When the big day arrived, my wife and I went to the auto show to find a big crowd around a draped car. George had invited the press and it was really a big happening. (The week before, *People Magazine*, had done a story on the custom-built Barrister automobile and the fact that movie stars and celebrities were buying them.) George presented me with a plaque along with a gold-plated tire gauge.

With that, he yanked the drape off the car and, much to my shock and dismay, I hated the color. It was very gaudy with gold-plated wire wheels and a gold painted body. I tried my best to hide my disappointment. If I had my choice, I would have had the paint job and the upholstery understated.

But as I thought about it, I realized that George Barris was the man who had invented the candy-apple paint job for cars. He was a car-customizer, that was his style, that's what had made him famous. However, while it might have been good for the movies and television, it was a little much to drive on the street. I called George aside and told him I was terribly unhappy with this choice of upholstery and paint and told him I wanted it redone. He told me it would cost another $8,000. I refused to drive the car.

I immediately put the car on a local car lot for sale and, typical of my luck, the custom car market fell apart just at that time. The car sat for over a year and I finally sold it for $28,000—a $22,000 loss on a car that I never drove.

Maybe I would have done better as a "Horse Trader!" I certainly could not have done any worse.

WANTED:
DEAD OR ALIVE

When I first came to Palm Springs in 1974, the police department had a reputation for taking care of the "locals." As the story went, if they found one of the citizenry drunk, instead of arresting them, they actually drove them home. The Police Chief was "one of the boys" and very accessible to everyone who lived in town.

It was the official opening of the social season in Palm Springs, always signified by the opening of the Racquet Club (the end of the season was signified by its closing.) My girlfriend and I were invited guests of some Racquet Club members and enjoyed a lovely evening of dining, dancing, socializing, and last but certainly not least, our fair share of imbibing. I was reasonably OK but my girlfriend was (as the saying goes) "three sheets to the wind!"

We were driving down Indian Avenue toward the Ingleside Inn at about 12:30 a.m. and as I passed the Howard Manor, a famous hotel in Palm Springs, I took my eyes off the road to see how many cars were in the parking lot (an occupational habit for restaurateurs). In front of the Howard Manor is a small, landscaped traffic island designed to turn all southbound traffic onto Palm Canyon Drive because Indian Avenue becomes a one way street there. I was driving a little two-seater Mercedes and because I wasn't paying attention, I jumped the island, damaging the undercarriage of my car.

Somehow I backed off the traffic island and started hobbling down Palm Canyon Drive at about ten miles per hour, hoping I would make it the twenty blocks to the Ingleside. About two blocks from the Ingleside, I was pulled over by the police. I was sure that it was obvious to them that the car was wobbling and they wanted to see if I needed help. The two officers walked up to the car and asked me to get out. I thanked them for their concern and assured them that everything was OK. They repeated their demand that I get out of the car and as soon as I did they grabbed my arms, turned me around, and handcuffed me! With that, another police car pulled up and ordered me to get in the back of the police car. My girlfriend was half unconscious and I said I couldn't leave her there alone. I was then pushed into the back seat of the police car which had a mesh screen separating me from the officers in front. I hollered to the first police car that they couldn't leave my girlfriend there, in her condition, especially at that time of night, with a disabled car. It was to no avail. I was taken to the police station, fingerprinted and booked on a charge of "destroying public property." I had no idea what they were talking about. Ironically, that very day, the Chief of Police and I had lunch in my restaurant.

I had no doubt that the whole event was a result of my drinking too much and that I would soon waken to find that this was all a bad dream. After they booked me, they took away my belt so I wouldn't kill myself (it must have been a pretty important piece of public property!) and locked me up in a cell.

After what seemed like a year, but was probably two hours, my manager showed up and arranged for my release. By this time it was 4:30 a.m. and my girlfriend was waiting at the hotel for me. It seems she sobered up rather quickly, left the car on the street, walked two blocks to the Inn, and called the manager and told him what happened. The manager was a personal friend of the Chief of Police. He called him at home and arranged to have me released.

I went home to get some sleep—feeling absolutely numb. I was awakened at about 10 a.m. by a phone call from a friend inquiring as to what happened. I asked him how he knew and he told me it was in the newspaper and all over the radio! I immediately called the Chief to find out where I stood. He asked me to come down to the police station to discuss the situation.

I was immediately ushered into his office and noticed that he wasn't the 'friend' I had lunch with the day before, but rather he was very aloof, impersonal and professional. Very coldly, he said that if I did not make an issue out of it the paperwork regarding the entire episode would disappear from the records as if nothing had ever happened. He did not want to discuss it at all. Not knowing what my options were, I told him I would get back to him. Considering all the negative publicity that had already occurred I consulted my attorney as to whether I should demand a public apology or sue the city for false arrest. My attorney advised that I forget the whole matter reminding me that it was a small town and that I intended to live and work here for a long time.

It became a local joke that I was the dangerous criminal that had assaulted public property.

There is an interesting sidelight to this incident. Approximately 18 months later, a friend of mine, who was in the security business, called to tell me that the F.B.I. was investigating me and had asked him a lot of questions about me. I was shocked to say the least! He said he had a connection there and would try to find out what it was all about.

It turned out that a shady character was spending a lot of time in my restaurant and the F.B.I. was checking to see if there was any connection to me. Upon checking the local police records and finding nothing, they were sure that I was a big-time gangster, based on the fact they knew I had been arrested (remember, my public property incident had been a big story in the local newspaper and on local radio) and apparently I had been able to make my file disappear. The assumption was that you had to be well connected to make your police record disappear. I can only guess that upon further investigation they found out I was really only "a small time hood!"

The next milestone in my criminal career occurred about eight years later. I was driving home one night at 2 a.m. from a disco I owned when I was pulled over by a police car. I had had a few drinks and was seriously concerned as to whether I would pass a sobriety test even though I felt totally competent to drive. It turned out to be a female police officer who asked for my driver's license and registration. I never carried a wallet so I knew I didn't have my license, but I was hoping there was some registration for the car in the glove compartment. As I was fumbling through the contents of the glove box the officer asked me to hand her a round, cosmetic looking tube that was in the glove box. I handed her the tube and continued fumbling for the registration which I finally found and I gave it to her.

She went back to her car, I assumed to check on my car's registration. After what seemed like forever, but was probably only fifteen-minutes, the officer returned and said, "Are you aware that carrying tear gas is a felony?" I asked her what she was talking about and she repeated that carrying tear gas was a felony. I asked her what that had to do with me, and she replied that the tube I had handed her was tear gas. I told her that I had no idea what she was talking about, that I had never seen the tube before, and probably had never even opened the glove compartment before. I said the tube was probably in there when I bought the car. She wrote me a ticket for carrying tear gas. I was greatly relieved that I had not gotten a 502 drunk-driving citation and could not believe my luck, as I knew a 502 was serious business, and this tear gas thing had to be a farce. When I got home, my girlfriend was waiting and worried.

Because it was now 3 a.m. in the morning and she was sure I had an accident, I said "You cannot believe this but with all the times I have driven home after a few drinks, tonight I got cited for tear gas possession. I don't even know where the dumb thing came from." My girlfriend said, "Is that were I left it?" She said she had looked all over for it, and had simply forgot that she had borrowed my car for a few days. She said she had it for several years and it has been originally given to her by a friend who was a policeman—before it was illegal to carry. I felt a lot better since I could explain to the police how it came to be in my glovebox.

The next day there were headlines in the local paper, front page no less, "Local Restaurateur Arrested on Felony Charges of Carrying Concealed Tear Gas!" In case you couldn't read, they made sure it was on the radio and TV newscasts every half hour. In addition to it being very embarrassing, it was an insult to my manhood to infer that I was carrying tear gas to protect myself. I called the Chief of Police and explained the situation. He said that there was nothing he could do at this point, as it was too public, and that I would have to go to trial. I really couldn't believe it was happening. It had to be a bad joke. I called my attorney who informed me that he did not handle felony cases and that I needed a criminal attorney. He recommended one to me and I set up an appointment for the next day.

When I met with the attorney he impressed on me that this was a very serious matter. He suggested that I line up as many character witnesses for the trial as I could find, such as the local Rabbi, Police Chief, Fire Chief, Mayor, etc. Knowing what kind of contributions I would have to make to repay their favorable testimony, I figured I would be better off with a $100,000 fine. The lawyer explained that the best strategy would be that after the police department tested the canister, we had a right to send it to an independent lab. The more times we sent the canister through the mail the better our chances would get that it would be lost and then there would be no case for lack of evidence.

I was given a trial date one month off and was anxiously awaiting the results of the police test hoping against hope that because my girlfriend had gotten it so long ago that it had become ineffective.

One day, as I was driving in my car, I heard on the news that the tear gas felony charge against restaurateur Mel Haber had been dropped for lack of evidence.

Who said crime doesn't pay!

LINE, SCHMINE WHO CARES?

I was in the middle of remodeling my house when it dawned on me that I was really building a completely new one. I originally bought the house in 1975. It was on a lovely and quiet street in Palm Springs. Real estate values were down that year and I made, what I considered, a good deal. The house was bordered on both sides by empty lots owned by the same man who had owned my house. As he was leaving town, he offered them to me for $20,000 apiece. Due to the fact that they were loaded with huge boulders, which I knew would make the lots too expensive to prepare for building, I passed on the deal (knowing no one else would buy them for the same reason).

About two years later I decided to add an office to the north side of my house and simply went ahead and did it without paying too much attention to where my property line was.

No sooner had the construction of my office been completed when a real estate broker I knew called to tell me that his client had just bought the lot to the north side of my house. He said a survey had revealed that my new office was one foot over the property line. He told me that I could either tear down my new office or try to buy the lot. He felt sure that his client would not be willing to sell me the one foot plus the legally required ten-foot setback. I really wanted to keep my office so I told him to check with his client to see how much he wanted for the lot. He came back with a price of $90,000. I couldn't believe it! I could have bought it for $20,000 just two years before.

After several sleepless nights I finally rationalized that it was a good investment for the future and, due to the fact that I was able to negotiate the price down $10,000 to $80,000, I went into escrow.

As I was picking up the final papers at the escrow office the lady casually mentioned, "Of course, you know the utility companies have an easement on the property line." I said, "What does that mean?" She replied, "Oh, it doesn't mean anything to you because you can't use the property line anyway because of the setbacks, however, it means that the utility companies have the right to go up the property line to access their equipment." I said, "Lady, I don't need the 160 feet I just bought, I only need one foot, and it's on the property line!" She replied, "Mister, I can't help you there, you will have to talk to the utility companies!"

I immediately called the electric company and found out that the head man happened to be a man whom I had met before. I rushed down to his office and started talking like a rapid-fire machine gun. I explained the situation—babbling that the property line had a building on it now and that they could not travel it to access their lines. But, I added, I would do anything to solve the problem. He insisted that they needed the easement so that they could service their lines. I said, "Sir, you don't understand! There is no more property line. I have a building sitting on it. However, I will even give you a key to my house so you can go through my house any time you have to access those lines…but you *can't* go up the property line because it no longer exists!"

We went back and forth for about twenty minutes while I tried to make my point. I was in a complete panic. I had just paid $80,000 to buy a lot 160 feet wide, because I needed just one foot, only to find that I could use the 159 feet I didn't need, but couldn't use the one foot I did need! The boss from the utility company said he would see what he could do and would call me back as soon as he could.

Finally, after three very anxious days, he called and said that under the circumstances, and the fact that I was a prominent member of the community, they would make a exception for me and give me back their easement, based on the fact that they could access their lines by every other property line on the street.

I was so grateful that I offered to make a contribution to his favorite charity, an offer he accepted and which I was more than happy to deliver.

I had recently married and decided to build my dream house. By this time I had acquired the lot on the south side of my house, so I now owned three adjacent lots. Behind my land was approximately ten acres of raw hillside owned by the famous composer Fritz Lowe (*My Fair Lady, Brigadoon*, etc. etc.). Mr. Lowe lived on the other side of this land which was actually in the next canyon. This land was (and still is as of this writing) rugged terrain and loaded with huge boulders.

My new house was beautifully designed and, in spite of all the problems that automatically accompany construction, it was an exciting project. In our enthusiasm we decided to build a beautiful waterfall at the side of the house which backed up to the Lowe property. It was an expensive project but was to be the focal point of our Shangri La. It took two men 90 days of moving and placing huge boulders, but was worth it. It was something to see and we were thrilled at the result.

About a week after the waterfall was finished, my wife called me at work to say that a man and woman had just traipsed across the rugged terrain of the adjacent land to look at our waterfall and were taking pictures of it. I felt flattered that people had heard how great it was and were actually coming just to see it.

Three days later I received a phone call from a man who introduced himself as Fritz Lowe's attorney. He said that Mr. Lowe would like to see a survey of my property so he could see where my waterfall was situated in relation to his property line. Having just completed a survey prior to starting the construction it did not seem like a big deal.

I called the engineer and asked him to locate the waterfall on my survey. Lo and behold, one corner of the waterfall was over my property line by about four feet. I immediately contacted the contractor to find out how this happened. He reminded me that I had insisted where the corner of the waterfall was to start and the stakes had indicated we were right on the property line. I realized it didn't matter how it happened at this stage, but how could I correct the problem now.

I submitted the survey to the attorney, not knowing what to expect, but not overly concerned about four feet in the corner of ten empty acres. One week later I received a phone call from the attorney informing me that they wanted me to move the waterfall off their property. I couldn't believe it! I asked for Mr. Lowe's phone number so that I could speak with him personally. The attorney told me that he couldn't give it to me and that I had 30 days to comply with the request. I was in total shock. I started calling around to various people I knew to find someone who was friendly with Fritz Lowe and could put me in contact with him. I finally found a mutual friend who informed me that Mr. Lowe has been mentally incompetent for quite awhile, incapable of handling his affairs, but his female companion took care of everything. I was given her name and promptly called their attorney and asked him to please put me in contact with her. He said he would call her and get back to me.

He called back two hours later and said she did not want to speak with me and she had directed him to tell me to just move the waterfall off their property. I truly thought I was going to have a heart attack. Firstly, I had no idea how to move a waterfall; secondly, I was sure the expense would be horrendous; and thirdly, I loved my waterfall just where it was!

Next I called around town to find someone who knew this lady. Several people did but nobody felt they could help me because she was known as a real "tough cookie." I was beside myself with frustration because I was unable to discuss the situation with anybody but the attorney.

Mr. Lowe's companion had an oddball last name and all of a sudden I remembered a famous Hollywood agent with the same last name who used to come into my restaurant. On a long shot I called the local Hollywood gossip columnist to find out if there was any connection. She said absolutely there was and that the lady was the famous agent's daughter. I called Hollywood information for the agent's telephone number. I called and asked for him, wondering if he would remember me. He was out just then but within fifteen minutes I received a return call from him. I began to feel a little better when he gave me a very cordial hello. He said that he definitely remembered me, and even apologized for not having been in the restaurant for a while, but explained that he had not been down to the 'Springs.'

I went through my long tale of woe about the waterfall and asked him if he could please put in a good word for me with his daughter—maybe even arrange a meeting with her and me. He said that his daughter had a mind of her own but that he would certainly try. I felt better now, at least having the possibility of some personal connection with this woman.

I called the building contractor, who was a personal friend, and told him the status of the situation. The contractor had once been a very notable figure in Hollywood and had created a prominent record company. He was literally a legend in the music business. He said that he didn't recognize the agent's name but there was a good chance the agent knew of him from his days in show business. He said that if the agent or his daughter did not call back within two days, he would take a shot and call the agent. Meanwhile, my "waterfall saga" was the topic of conversation at my restaurant. Anybody who would listen was told of my tale of woe. I was milking the story for all it was worth…"How's your waterfall?" became the standard question.

Two days after I spoke to the agent, I finally received a call from his daughter. She started off very coldly and said, "Mr. Haber, I understand you want to talk to me." Very humbly, I thanked her for calling and then broke into this impassioned plea to allow me to keep the waterfall where it was. She responded, "We would just like you to move your waterfall off our property." I said, "Miss, we made a mistake. I would be more than happy to buy the four feet the waterfall is over the property line for any amount you think would be fair." She repeated that they just wanted me to move it. I tried another tack. "The waterfall doesn't hurt your property, if anything, it enhances your property. It looks good and if it doesn't hurt anything why not just leave it? As a matter of fact, I will give you a letter stating that I will remove the waterfall any time you want, but it makes no sense to tear it down now." She just repeated, "We just want you to move your waterfall!" I pleaded, "Miss, this is a small town and we have a lot of mutual friends (I named everybody I could think of)." I added jokingly,

"You can eat for free in my restaurant for the rest of your life…but please, let me keep my waterfall!" She said, "We just want you to move your waterfall." I felt as though I were talking to a recording! Desperate, I took my last shot and said, "Look, I don't really have to own the waterfall, I really just want to look at it, so why don't I just give you the portion of my land that it's sitting on. I will maintain it but you will own it. This way you could tear it down any time you want!" And her response?…"We just want you to move your waterfall." Twenty minutes of begging, cajoling, and coercing finally convinced me that I had run into an absolute brick wall. The conversation ended as coldly as it had begun.

Totally frustrated, I called my contractor friend and told him what happened. He said, "Give me her father's number and I'll take a shot at this." Thirty minutes later he called back and I could hear the excitement in his voice. He told me that not only did the agent know who he was, but he gave my friend a greeting like he was a long lost friend. The agent said that he had just recently been talking about him and wondered what had happened to him after he left show business. My friend felt the agent could not have been friendlier.

My contractor friend said they spent twenty minutes together on the phone discussing great stories from the past, as well as the many mutual clients which my friend had recorded on his record label. My friend explained to the agent that after selling his record company for big money, he went to Iran to build an entire city for the Shah. When the Shah's regime fell, my friend lost all of his money. He came back to the States and became a building contractor. He told the agent that he was the contractor for the waterfall that his daughter wanted moved. He explained that if the waterfall had to be moved it would have to come out of his pocket. He asked the agent, for "old times' sake," to please talk to his daughter. He said he felt that she couldn't have a heart of stone and if her father could explain the whole situation to her that she would see reason. My friend was totally optimistic as he told me about the conversation and said the agent promised to call back within 24 hours. I felt as though I had finally found the "key to this lock."

Two days passed and no word from the agent. My friend couldn't understand it and called the agent's office and left a message. My friend called four more times over the next two days with the same result. We finally figured out that we had been doing great until he told the agent he had gone broke in Iran. How quickly they forget! It became obvious to us that once the agent knew my friend was no longer a big power broker, there was absolutely no reason to put himself out.

After living with this anxiety for 30 days , it finally dawned on me that the situation did not involve matters of life and death but was only a matter of dollars.

I finally moved the waterfall and I must tell you that the ironic payoff is that it looks much better, and far more dramatic, four feet closer to the house!

P.S. Fritz Lowe passed away six months after I moved the water-fall and his property was sold .

All's well that ends well.

BUSMAN'S HOLIDAY

W ell, I was ready for a much needed rest. A few days in Mexico sounded just perfect. I loved Puerto Vallarta, but since I had been there many times before, my wife wanted us to go somewhere I'd never been so it would always be "our special place."

We chose Mazatlan, and with great excitement, booked a four-day stay at the top hotel there. We flew out of San Diego, and even though our flight was delayed for two hours, our enthusiasm was not dampened—if anything, it was heightened. The flight was marred by a great deal of turbulence —requiring three straight Beefeater Gin drinks to keep me from shaking. I had become a 'white knuckle' flyer in my old age. I knew that I had drunk enough when I began rooting for the plane to go down! I was sure the pilot had vertigo because the plane flew at a 45 degree angle the whole way.

It seemed like an endless wait for our luggage to arrive. In reality, it never did arrive! The airline assured us that it would be on the next flight due to arrive in two hours. They suggested that we check into our hotel and when the luggage arrived they would deliver it to us there.

We were hot and tired and just wanted to bathe and rest. We jumped into a cab and about half way there, the cab broke down and the driver couldn't get it started again. He told us that we were lucky that we didn't have any luggage to carry. We trudged the few remaining blocks to the hotel and checked in at the front desk. The bellman escorted us to our room and opened the door — revealing a couple in bed. After profuse apologies, the manager assured us that it would only require a couple of minutes to straighten out the problem. We waited in the lobby for over thirty minutes. Finally, we were taken to another room. I called room service and ordered a couple of sandwiches to tide us over until dinner. After taking our baths, we dozed off. When we awoke, I realized that it had been two hours since I had ordered the sandwiches. I called room service again and was told that they had closed an hour ago. Next, I called the airport to find out when our luggage would arrive—only to hear that it had not arrived on the flight following ours. They said we should buy whatever we needed to have right away. After hanging up, I knew that this was not going to be the greatest of my vacation experiences.

We went out to get a bite to eat and to buy the toiletries we needed to last until our luggage showed up. By this time it was evening and we called it a day—hoping the following one would be better.

Early the next morning we got up and called the airline again; still, no luck with our luggage—they were nowhere to be found. We bought a couple of bathing suits in the hotel's store and headed for the pool. There was not one empty lounge chair in the pool area and it was so crowded that there was hardly room to walk around. We discovered that it was Cinco de Mayo, the Mexican equivalent of Independence Day. Unable to find any space there, we went to the beach and eventually found two chaise lounges. We weren't too far from the parachute ride that is typical to most Mexican beaches. I had been on this type of ride several times before and found it quite exciting. They hook you up in a parachute that is towed by boat out over the ocean. It's very exhilarating and the view is magnificent from a few hundred feet up.

I paid the fee, was hooked up and we were off. About ten minutes into the ride, the boat slowed down and I began to descend into the water. I assumed they would start to pick up speed again and I would go right back up. Wrong! The boat came to a complete stop and I wound up smack in the middle of the ocean. I immediately wriggled out of the parachute harness and started to tread water. The boat was about two hundred yards away but I couldn't see any activity. I started to swim toward it, but since I was a heavy smoker, I had to rest every few strokes by floating on my back. When I was about half way to the boat, I saw another boat towing it away! No one made any effort to find me or see if I was okay! About forty five minutes later, I reached the shore to find my wife running frantically up and down the beach screaming for someone to help...to no avail.

I rested for a few minutes and went over to the people who ran the parachute ride and complained about what had transpired—I had been totally abandoned with absolutely no concern for my well-being. The boss looked at me calmly and said, "Señor, you want your money back?"

We spent the rest of the day on the beach not daring to do anything other than stroll to the ocean to cool off. We had reservations at a local restaurant for dinner but first checked with the airline about our luggage—still no luck. We went to a local boutique and bought two inexpensive outfits just to get by. We ate early and returned to our room to get a good night's rest.

Three hours later my wife came down with the famous "Montezuma's Revenge." She was in bad shape. She had tremendous stomach pain and I was trying to comfort her—when the power went out. I called the front desk to find out what was happening and how long it would last and was told that it happened all the time but that it didn't usually take more than two hours to fix. That was the last straw! We decided that the gods did not want us in Mexico. I called the airline and got the only two remaining seats on the only flight leaving the next day. We didn't get much sleep that night but were looking forward to getting home to our own bed.

When we arrived at the airport we were informed that our flight had been delayed four hours. Rather than wait there we decided to go back to the hotel and get some rest while waiting. No surprise, our room had already been rented and they didn't have another one available. We had no choice but to go back to the airport and wait. My wife got "loaded" on dramamine to keep her stomach quiet and I got "loaded" on Beefeater Gin. We both then fell asleep at the airport, completely missed our flight out and spent the next twenty four hours at the Mazatlan airport.

Needless to say, we are still looking for a new 'Shangri-la!'

P.S. It is now ten years later and we have been assured that our missing luggage will be on the next flight.

ASPEN

S omewhere at the beginning of a relationship with a new girlfriend, she suggested a short skiing trip to Aspen, Colorado. At
this point I must mention that to a Jewish boy from Brooklyn, a
skiing holiday was as alien as snow would be to a camel or as the desert
would be to a polar bear.

All my vacations were automatically to warm, sunny climates
such as Puerto Rico, Miami Beach, Acapulco, Las Vegas, Palm
Springs, or Los Angeles. It had taken me 35 years to master the art of
exactly when you turn over in the sun from your stomach to your back,
so as to have a perfectly even sun tan and not get over-cooked on one
side or the other.

At first I was absolutely appalled by the idea, but upon careful
consideration, I thought it might be a kick. The other incentive for
this trip was the idea that Aspen was where the 'Beautiful People'
went, and having never seen any, I wanted to investigate first-hand.

Based on the fact that I was going from a cold New York climate
to a colder Colorado climate, I made all the arrangements with great
trepidation. My lady had lived in Aspen for several years and skiing
was her whole life. I had read about people like that but had never
been personally exposed to them.

She was very excited as we planned a four-day jaunt. A week
later we flew in to Denver, Colorado, where the temperature was ten
degrees below zero, and where we were going to spend the night as
planes didn't fly into Aspen after dark. The whole concept of this trip
was alien to me but I went along to see what it was all about.

The following morning we were to fly from Denver to Aspen,
Colorado. It was a small commuter airline which serves Aspen, and
had been aptly named Aspen Scareways. I had heard often that once
you visit Aspen you never leave it. To me, a flight on Aspen Scareways
would explain that. I had never been the world's greatest flying enthusiast but I had brought along a bottle of Beefeater Gin purposely to
make my flights more enjoyable.

As the people deplaned the incoming flight from Aspen, I overheard several people comment that the trip had been exceptionally bumpy. I immediately ran into the men's room and took three stiff belts of gin in order to enhance my 'enjoyment.' We then boarded, what at that time was, the smallest plane I had ever been on. It was my good fortune to get the last seat on the plane whereupon the stewardess promptly informed me that she had been flying this route for ten years and the flight just in from Aspen was the bumpiest she had ever experienced. She obviously had not gotten an "A" in her "How to Comfort a Passenger" class.

I would like to describe the plane. Upon boarding, you cannot stand up because the plane is not high enough inside. There are no bathrooms aboard and the door to the pilot's compartment...does not exist. As soon as you are seated, they explain how to use the oxygen as chances are you will have to use it the entire trip. Aspen Scareways justifiably deserves its name. The plane does not fly into Aspen—it literally bounces in. If you've ever seen a chart of a cardiograph, it's similar to the flying pattern of those airplanes. They are either up or down and never flying level. I wasn't sure whether the gin distiller had made a mistake and put water in the bottle instead of alcohol because half a bottle later I seemed to be just as nervous as I was when I started drinking it.

After what seemed like 3½ years, we finally landed at Aspen airport. The airport was so small in those days that when you went to the men's room, you actually locked the door behind you. How quaint! Considering all I had heard and read about this world-renowned ski resort, the airport certainly seemed to be a bit understated.

I must admit the weather was cool, crisp and beautiful. I had seen many pictures of people skiing in bathing suits, and one of my goals was to witness this phenomenon. Everyone in Brooklyn knew that cold weather was uncomfortable and I would prove this for my friends (and myself, I might add) once and for all. On top of that, I had seen ads claiming that people could get sunburns while skiing. That, if true, would certainly shoot the hell out of my theory that Miami

Beach was the best place to get a suntan.

We taxied to a condominium we had reserved and settled in. Next, my lady took me to a ski shop in town, rented all the appropriate equipment for me, purchased the essential clothing and I was enrolled in a beginners ski class for the following morning at 9 a.m. We returned to the condominium where I got all decked out in my new ski clothes. At this point, I must tell you that every picture I had ever seen of anybody in ski clothes made all the men look like Greek Gods and the women like Swiss beauties. I have never seen anybody in ski clothes who did not look healthy and beautiful and I was pretty proud of myself as I stared in the mirror at the new Melvyn, realizing that this was probably the best I would ever look.

Feeling super, and wanting to show off, I asked, "Where do the beautiful people have lunch?" My lady replied, "Why, Andre's, of course." Of Course! Aspen, being the small town it is, we set out to walk the 2½ blocks to Andre's. During the short walk, my lady greeted several old friends in the street and I was beginning to enjoy this new world.

As we entered Andre's Restaurant, I glanced around the room and noticed groups of young, good-looking people, all seemingly having a great time. After an appropriate welcome by the owner, who was an old friend of my lady's, we were seated at a table in the rear of the restaurant. Wanting desperately to do everything in character, I allowed my lady to order for me whatever it is the beautiful people would have for lunch in such a place.

As we were chatting, I noticed a couple in the front of the restaurant staring at us —to the point of being rude. I was beginning to feel very uncomfortable as it was obvious that they had something on their minds. About halfway through the meal, the couple got up and approached our table. The man introduced himself and explained that they were from *Women's Wear Daily* (a very popular garment center newspaper) and were doing a feature article on the beautiful people in the various ski resorts. They had just come from Sun Valley and Vail,

Colorado. They had been in Aspen two days and said that we were the first beautiful people they had seen here and would we mind being photographed for the article. I cannot describe my reaction, as I had come all this way just to observe the beautiful people, and here I was being told that I was the beautiful people. (I was never quite sure what that really meant.)

My lifestyle in New York City, regarding exercise, consisted entirely of none. The most energetic act that I would attempt in the course of a normal day would be to try and sit up straight in my office chair. Here I was, a smoker of four packs a day, plodding around Aspen, 6,000 feet above sea level. I considered it quite a feat just to be able to walk, which is how we spent the rest of the day.

My gal had been reasonably well-known in town during the period she had lived there. During the course of my visit in Aspen, I became affectionately known as "look-at-the-depths-Beverly-has-fallen-to." I thought it was cute, even though it was rather a long name for me, it did give me an identity all my own.

The following morning I was delivered to a beginner's ski class consisting of 9-year-old children, 17-year-old girls and a 60-year-old widow. I must tell you it did not serve my ego well. I was put on these tiny skis and told that only falling three times in the first fifteen feet was a great accomplishment for someone who had never been on skis. Statistics showed that the first time on skis, beginners fell at least four times in the first fifteen feet.

I began to get my self-confidence back. I spent my first two mornings in this class twisting, turning, falling down, helping my 9-year-old classmates to their feet and consoling my 60-year old widowed classmate, while my gal went off skiing with the real "hot dogs." At the end of the second day, Beverly informed me that I was ready to go to the top of Ajax mountain. Not really having any idea what Ajax was, but sensing it would be an accomplishment, I eagerly awaited the opportunity to go where the "real" skiers went.

That night, we dined at one of the local restaurants and everytime an acquaintance of my lady's came by she would mention that little *Melvyn had only taken two lessons and tomorrow was going up to the top of Ajax Mountain*. For some reason I was too dumb to pick up on everybody's surprise and amazement. I certainly would understand it the following day. Quite pleased with the anticipation of the great adventure that awaited me in the morning, and totally fatigued from twisting and turning on the beginner's mountain, I slept rather peacefully that night.

The following morning at 9 o'clock, we had breakfast in the Lodge at the foot of the mountain known as Ajax. We put on our ski gear and got in the line for the chairlift. Now anyone who has done any skiing at all is aware of the relatively simple task of properly getting on the ski chair. This was going to be my first test with the 'big people' and I certainly wanted to look like Mr. Cool.

I waited on the skilift line impatiently and finally it was my time to jump into position for the chair. Needless to say, after one step I fell flat on my face and everybody hollered at me to stay down while the chair lift passed right over my head. It sure beat taking the chance of having my head lopped off. Finally, after Mr. Cool was helped up by three people, they managed to get me on the chair lift. I had no idea where I was going, but I am sure, sitting on that chair lift, no one could tell me apart from the other people in the chairs who knew where they were going and what they were doing.

Quite some time went by—I would guess about 30 to 35 minutes. By now we were on our third chair lift and still going straight up. It was at that point that I turned around and saw the city of Aspen directly beneath me. The only time I had been so high was inside an airplane. I was really beginning to enjoy this sport as the ride up was a lot of fun, and I had experienced no suffering or exhaustion to this point. Skiing was really a rather easy sport, I thought. As the chair lift came to the debarkation point, Mr. Cool got off the chair as instructed and, you guessed it, Mr. Cool went face down in the snow.

Fortunately, the people who got off the chair behind us were experienced skiers, used to skiing around clods like me lying in the snow. As I got up I attempted to recover my pride by announcing out loud, "My ski must have hit a rock or something."

At that point, we skiied down a little hill at the top of the mountain several times, and I must admit it was not too bad. By this time it was 1 o'clock in the afternoon and I was advised that this was cocktail time at the Lodge at the top of Ajax and all the people that counted congregated up there to eat, drink and be merry. We went to the Lodge where Beverly seemed to know everybody. We promptly joined a group of people. We sat around chatting at how good the powder was. It seemed a lot easier to talk the game than to play the game.

Several very enjoyable hours passed and somebody mentioned that a storm was coming and perhaps it was time to ski down the mountain. We went outside and it was blowing and snowing like crazy. I suddenly realized that the one piece of equipment that I had failed to purchase was a pair of goggles.

After getting down the tiny hill at the top, the runs started to become much tougher, and considering I could not see where I was going in the blizzard, I started to fall consistently. The combination of not having any stamina to begin with, not being able to ski, a blizzard, no goggles and darkness setting in, I was feeling certain anxieties that I had never experienced before. It seemed that it was my misfortune that every time I fell, I fell off to the side of the main ski trail. When I attempted to pick myself up by pushing against the ground, my arms would go into the soft snow about 4 feet deep and I could get no leverage to push myself up. At this point, I was beginning to suffer extreme exhaustion. Everytime I would fall, I would ask my girlfriend how much further, and she would answer, "Only a little bit further." It got to a point where I would stand up and try to fall forward in the hopes that I could gain some ground simply by tumbling down the hill.

For what seemed to me like six months and two hundred miles later, I started to genuinely fear for my life. The bottom of the mountain was nowhere in sight. It seemed like I did not have one ounce of energy left. I was frozen stiff and I was spending more time in the snow than out of it. I couldn't even feel my face. My hair was one solid icicle. I was covered from top to bottom with ice, and now it was really getting dark and the blizzard was increasing. By now there were several passing skiers who were in quite a hurry to get off the mountain right away. My lady friend tried to enlist their help in finding the ski patrol. At this point, I secretly prayed for death to relieve my ordeal. I had never experienced the combination of anxiety, fear and terror simultaneously before.

I literally tumbled down that mountain inch by inch. I believe the height is 8,000 feet and every inch of it was covered by the body of Melvyn Haber during my trip down. Finally, I reached the bottom where several people carried me to our condominium, which fortunately was only half a block from the base of the mountain.

To give you an idea how bad it was, I skied in a warm-up suit over jeans and when they put me in front of the fireplace, it took the cuffs of my jeans over half an hour for the ice to thaw out. I laid there semi-conscious for the next few hours in a total state of shock. I subsequently came to learn that Ajax is the most challenging mountain for advanced skiers in Aspen, Colorado. When I finally got my senses back, my companion made the understatement of the year when she said, "I guess you weren't quite ready for Ajax."

THE NANNY

I became very friendly with a guest of my hotel who was from London, England. He was an outrageous character, which is another story. He had the ability to make himself known to anybody and everybody within ten minutes. He had spent a considerable amount of time at the Ingleside Inn and after he returned to London he called me monthly and begged me to come for a visit as his house guest. At one point, I actually made plans to go. I organized my passport, ordered an airplane ticket, bought travelers checks, and even started to pack, but changed my mind. I was on sort of a "bummer."I had just broken up with my girlfriend and thought I needed a change of scenery, but really didn't know what I wanted to do. I called my English friend, Leslie, and told him I was depressed and had changed my mind and decided not to go. I told him that as soon as my head straightened out I would come over for a visit.

About three weeks passed, it was a Saturday night and I had been drinking pretty good. A friend of mine from Los Angeles, who was staying with me for the weekend, suggested I return to L.A. with him. On a wild impulse, I decided I would go with him to L.A. and have him drop me off at the Los Angeles Airport and fly to London. The idea of going at a moment's notice really excited me. I threw some things in my valise, grabbed my passport and travelers checks and jumped into his car.

When I arrived at the airport, I bought a ticket to London and called Leslie and told him I would be arriving the following (Monday) morning at 8 a.m. He said he would be there to pick me up with "bells on"! I called my manager in Palm Springs and told him I would be back in a week. I had a few cocktails on the plane and slept through most of the flight.

Leslie was anxiously waiting as I deplaned at Heathrow airport. He was waving a *London Daily Mirror* newspaper at me and, after we hugged each other, he showed me an article in the previous day's newspaper about me. There were three pictures of me with different celebrities in a half-page story about the Ingleside Inn and Melvyn's

Restaurant. (It was a million-to-one shot that it appeared the day before my first visit to London. I had been interviewed by the reporter three months before.) It was a pretty good start for my holiday.

I was exhausted so we went for a bite to eat and Leslie took me to his apartment to take a nap and get refreshed. He had a lovely one-bedroom apartment and insisted that I sleep in his bed and he would sleep on the couch in the living room.

After a brief nap and shower, I was ready for the London night-life. Leslie took me to the three most exclusive private clubs, intro-ducing me as the most famous hotelier in America, and showing the newspaper article to everybody to prove it. I was given the red carpet treatment and really enjoyed playing the celebrity. We must have visited half the clubs in London until it was daylight. We dragged ourselves back to his apartment and I quickly fell asleep.

I was soon to discover that Leslie is one of those people that never sleeps. When I awoke at noon, Leslie was dressed and ready to go out for lunch. I was feeling alone and depressed and declared that I was going to make plans to go home the following day. (It is not unusual for me to go someplace planning to stay for a week or two and return home in two days.)

Leslie told me that he had made reservations at the "in" place for lunch. It was a typical dreary, rainy, depressing London day, and it sure didn't help my mood. We took a taxi to the heart of London where the restaurant was located. He certainly picked a great place as it was packed with "beautiful people." I recognized several movie stars, and all the ladies looked like the fashion models from Fifth Avenue in New York City. Leslie made sure that the owner was aware of how impor-tant I was and we were given one of the best tables.

After Leslie had greeted half the people in the restaurant, we finally settled down to order. Two people came in whom I knew from Palm Springs. Jimmy was a personal friend of mine and his friend was the famous, international financier, Bernie Cornfeld, whom I had met before through Jimmy. (At one time, Bernie had six or seven castles and homes throughout Europe and Jimmy traveled the world with him as his companion.) They joined us for lunch and Bernie asked when I was going back to the States. I told him I planned to return the following day, Wednesday. He suggested that I wait until Friday and fly back with them. Bernie invited Leslie and I to go out with him and Jimmy that evening. He suggested that we meet at his house, play backgammon for an hour or two (we both loved backgammon and we had played each other before), and then go out for dinner and to some of the clubs. It sounded great to me and I sure had nothing better to do.

Bernie lived on the most fashionable street in London, in a beautiful three-story townhouse. He gave us the complete tour, including a full-blown disco in the basement. It was definitely set up to be a party house. We played a little backgammon and went out to dinner and visited several private clubs where Bernie was treated like royalty. It really was a super evening and I was glad I had run into them. We agreed to meet again the following evening.

Thursday, Leslie showed me around London during the day. We arrived at Bernie's house at about 6 p.m. and discovered six young ladies sitting in the living room while Bernie was in the corner on the telephone. I sensed something strange, a sort of tension in the air. Everybody seemed uncomfortable. I saw Jimmy in the next room and asked him what was going on. He told me that somewhere along the way Bernie had gotten married and had a young daughter. She was about to spend a couple of months with him, so he had advertised for a nanny to take back to the States to take care of his daughter. Employment opportunities in England were extremely tough at that time so Bernie had received over 100 resumes and picked these 6 girls to interview. So the tension I sensed was due to the fact that these girls were competing with each other for the job.

I felt out of place and told Bernie that since he was busy we should just meet at the airport in the morning. Bernie said, "Nonsense, how would you like the best prime rib in London?" I said it sounded great. Leslie, Jimmy, Bernie, I, and the six nanny candidates walked down the street to the famous Claridges' Hotel. Bernie had called ahead and they had set up a long table in the middle of the dining room for us.

I was seated between Leslie and a lovely young English girl. All this little girl wanted to know was whether or not I could help her get the nanny job. Apparently, she had worked in the States before and would do anything to go back. She had an adorable accent and I felt kind of sorry for her.

I was drinking pretty good and about half way through the meal I turned to the girl and said that if she really wanted to go to the States so badly, I would take her as my guest. She looked at me for a moment and then asked, "What would I have to do?" I said, "First, let's establish the fact that I am not flying you to the States to sleep with you!" She then asked the obvious question, "Then why would you do it?" I said, "Because everybody will ask me what I brought back from London, and I will say a little English nanny." I explained that the fun I would have with the story was worth the price of the airplane ticket. She said, "I do believe you are serious." I said, "Young lady, there is nothing to believe. Tomorrow you will either be on a plane to America or not." She said she was getting very nervous and I told her to go home, pack, and meet me at Bernie's house at 9 a.m. and we would all go to the airport together.

She said, "I have two problems. I don't have a current passport and I have to tell my boss I'm leaving." I said, "I can't help you with those problems. Here's the phone number at Leslie's house where I'm staying. Call me in the morning if you are going."

After dinner, the girls left and Leslie, Bernie and I went out nightclubbing until the wee hours of the morning. The next thing I knew, Leslie was waking me to say that I had a phone call. It was 7:30 a.m. and the nanny was on the phone . She said, "Good morning, this is Annie. I am at the passport office and will meet you at Bernie's house." I had to shake the cobwebs out of my head to remember the previous night's conversation. After remembering my bravado of the night before, I decided to honor my commitment. I quickly dressed, grabbed my suitcase and Leslie drove me to Bernie's house. I had been there about 15 minutes before Annie arrived. (I must admit she looked adorable in a pair of tight fitting jeans and all of a sudden it dawned on me that this might even turn out to be a bonanza.) She dropped her suitcase and asked, "Where's the phone? I have to call my boss." She made her call in the kitchen and returned saying that she was all set and ready to go.

Considering that there were now four of us going to the airport, plus all of our luggage, and the fact that London taxis are small, Bernie called for two cabs. When the cabs arrived, I, being a gentlemen, went to pick up her luggage. She held up her hand to stop me and then proceeded to arrange with the driver to handle all of the luggage. I was impressed! We arrived at the airport and she made the arrangements to have our luggage brought to the ticket counter, arranged our tickets, and asked if I would care for anything. I responded that I would love to have a cocktail. I gave her some money and she ran off to fetch the drink. This really was not going to be very hard to take.

We boarded the plane. Annie sat next to me, Jimmy sat directly behind me and Bernie sat opposite of me in the stewardess's jump seat so that we could play backgammon. As soon as we were airborne, Annie got some magazines to read while Bernie and I started our backgammon tournament. About an hour into the flight, I accidentally bumped elbows with Annie and she gave me a very warm smile. That was the first contact of any kind between us.

We were about an hour out of Los Angeles when Bernie decided to get some rest before we landed. Bernie moved to the back of the plane and I put my seat back and started to think about my new "nanny." She was very cute and I found her adorable English accent very charming. I conjured up a picture of her in a little maid's uniform with a short skirt and little hat on her head. She turned to me and asked, "What would you like me to call you?" I replied, "You should call me Mr. Haber." She said, "You know Mr. Haber, I don't know how to drive a car." For a moment I didn't know what to say. Palm Springs was not like a big city where you could walk to the corner market or where there is public transportation to take you wherever you want to go. It definitely would be pretty tough to run a household and do all the chores required without driving a car. I realized I didn't have much of a choice at that point and I would just have to make the best of it. I figured I would have to get her a bicycle with a huge basket and that would be how she could run her errands. I explained my idea to her and she said that would be no problem. I figured that if she worked out I would ultimately teach her to drive.

She inquired about the living arrangements, and I explained that I lived in a large home, where she would have her own little corner of the house with her own bedroom, bath, and private entrance. I assured her that it would be a rather loose arrangement, that I was easy to get along with, and she only had to stay as long as she wanted. I felt excited by the whole situation. Then Annie said, "Mr. Haber, when we land I have to go through a different customs gate than you because I am not a citizen, and although I have a return plane ticket, I do need to show some cash to get through customs. Could you please lend me some until I clear immigration?" I gave her two one-hundred dollar bills.

We landed in Los Angeles and I was a mess, not having really slept in several days. When I got to the customs official I must have looked suspicious because he went through everything, including my tooth-paste. To make this even more embarrassing, Steve Martin, the famous comedian, was behind me and became impatient as the customs official was busy turning my socks inside out. I finally cleared customs and met up with everyone. Annie and I were walking about 25 feet ahead of Jimmy and Bernie through the long corridor that leads to the street.

As we approached the waiting area, I saw my ex-girlfriend waiting there. Our break-up had happened shortly before I had decided to go to London and I had no idea how she knew I was arriving on this flight. But there was no doubt that she was there waiting for me. Not knowing what to expect, I instinctively turned to Annie and said, "Go with Jimmy. He will explain everything." I ran over to my ex-girlfriend, gave her a kiss, and quickly left the airport with her.

She drove us to her home in Long Beach where we spent the night. The following morning, she drove me to Palm Springs. When I didn't invite her to move back in with me, she slapped my face, spit in my eye, said some unrepeatable things, and drove off in a huff.

I was still dragging from my international adventure. It was an unusually hot day and all I wanted to do was to get some sleep. I fell asleep for about four hours and awoke feeling much better. All of a sudden it dawned on me that somewhere in this wonderful country was a cute English nanny whose airfare I had paid and I had no idea where she was. I called Jimmy's house only to get an answering machine. I called L.A. information for Bernie's number but no luck. There was nothing more I could do. I figured sooner or later I would hear something from Jimmy.

The next day at about 6 p.m., as I was getting ready to go to the restaurant for a typically busy Saturday night, the hotel switchboard called to say that there was an Annie on the line. I answered and heard a cute English-accented voice say, "Mel, when am I going to see you?" It was the first time she had called me Mel and it sounded intimate, friendly and very interesting.

I asked her where she was and she said she was staying at Bernie's house (a mansion in the best part of Los Angeles). I asked what she had done the night before and she said, "Oh, we went to Hefner's house (the legendary Hugh Hefner of *Playboy* fame) for a party." Surprised at that, I asked who had been at the party and she named every big star...and then some. She said there had been about 100 people there. I asked what she had done today and she said, "I hope you won't mind, but I went shopping in Beverly Hills and spent your $200 on a pair of boots." I asked what she was going to do that night and she said that they had planned to go back to the Playboy mansion for another party! I said, "Wait a minute, you're staying in Bernie's mansion, partying at Hefner's and shopping in Beverly Hills. Why would you want to come to Palm Springs?" She replied, "The only reason I came to America was to be with you." I was really flabbergasted and quite flattered. I explained to her that since it was a Saturday night I would be too busy at the restaurant and couldn't spend any time with her anyway. I asked her to call me the following evening and we would discuss arrangements.

As fate would have it, my ex-girlfriend came into the restaurant that night and she looked sensational. We went out dancing and before I knew it we were back together. We drove back to her house in Long Beach the following morning, loaded up most of her clothing and she was my housemate once again.

About 5 p.m. Sunday afternoon, the switchboard called and said Annie was on the line. I told them to take a message and to say I was unavailable. There was no way I could see Annie now, but I really didn't feel too guilty when I considered where she was staying and what she was doing. Annie called the next three days in a row and not knowing what to say I simply ducked the phone calls. The fourth day her phone calls stopped and I knew she got the message.

About two weeks had passed when Bernie called and said, "Mel, I don't mind storing your furniture (referring to Annie) but it is time to have it moved." I asked what Annie had been doing for the past two weeks and Bernie said that she had had the time of her life. According to him, she partied every night and had managed to be with everybody, except the gardener, and that was only because he was sick and hadn't come to work. I said, "Bernie, just put her on a plane. She has a return ticket which I have already had paid for." Bernie said, "Mel, she cashed that in ten days ago." Needless to say, I sent Bernie the money to buy Annie a return ticket to London.

Somewhere in London is a darling little English nanny who I hope had the best two weeks of her life courtesy of the good samaritan Melvyn Haber. The only reason I am telling this story is because all I got for my money is the right to tell this tale. (Incidentally, my girlfriend moved out the day that Annie boarded her flight back to London!)

C'est la vie"!

VIGNETTES

The Ultimate In Personalization

When I first opened the Inn in 1975, I spent a lot of time and energy creating little custom touches to please my clientele. At that time, many of these little details did not exist in other hotels but have since become commonplace in many of them. One of these special touches was to put the guest's name on matchbook covers with the date of their arrival. We put one personalized matchbook in each ashtray in their room.

One day, the famous TV host, Ed McMahon, checked into the Ingleside Inn for a weekend stay. He made it a point to seek me out and courteously complimented me on all the personal touches; complimentary continental breakfast, complimentary snacks, a basket of fruit — and he was especially impressed by his name on the matches. He told me he had never seen that anywhere. I thanked him profusely for his appreciation.

Several hours later he called and said, "You have really outdone yourself now!" He said, "I don't know how you do it, but this certainly takes the cake. We just ordered room service and I really can't believe it." I had no idea what he was talking about but was determined not to let him know that. I asked one of my staff to see if they could discretely inquire as to what the "piece de resistance" had been.

It turned out that, with his room service order, he had ordered two cocktails which they served with on a napkin with a big "M" on it. It seems he assumed they had been personalized for him, not realizing that the "M" stood for "Melvyn's." Rather than destroy this impression, I immediately had all the "M" napkins removed from the restaurant and substituted plain napkins for the rest of his stay.

When You're Big, You're Big

I had just completed a two-month period during which I appeared on several national TV shows including the *David Susskind Show*, the *Phil Donahue Show*, and last but certainly not least, *60 Minutes*. One evening, I was at the bar in Melvyn's chatting with one of my customers who had seen the shows and who was asking if I had seen any benefit to my business as a result of all my TV exposure. I told him I really wasn't sure, but many people recognized me on the street and in various places. But, I guessed, it had to have some residual benefit to my hotel and restaurant. With that, a restaurant customer was passing by on the way to the men's room. He stopped, looked at me and said, "Hey, I recognize you. I just saw you on the *Phil Donahue Show*." I turned to my friend at the bar and gave him a smug look as if to say, I told you so. With that the gentleman said, "I thought you were very good. By the way, what do you do?"

When I first came to town I discovered that one of Palm Springs' old guard was a retired doctor, Norman Haber. His wife is a lovely lady, Minette and her car's personalized license plate is M. Haber. Frequently, people mentioned seeing me at various places because they had seen the car's license plate, M. Haber, and assumed it was me.

One day, Minette Haber was driving on the street behind the Ingleside Inn when her car backfired rather loudly and stalled right in the middle of the road. There was not much she could do, so she left the car in the middle of the street and came to the Inn to call the AAA. One of the neighbors, hearing the loud backfire, looked out the window and saw the car with the M. Haber license plate. The neighbor assumed that it was my car and that the loud noise had been a gun shot. She called the police and reported that Mel Haber had just been shot.

As Minette Haber and I were sitting in the restaurant, having a cup of coffee and waiting for the AAA, two cops rushed in and went straight to the Maitre d' to inform him that Mel Haber had just been shot. I almost had the chance to read my own obituary!

Several years ago a couple from an affluent community in Long Island, New York, dined at Melvyn's and absolutely loved it. They promised to tell all their friends back in New York.

About eight months later, their next door neighbors came to Palm Springs, stayed at the Canyon Hotel, and planned to visit Melvyn's Restaurant. The only problem was that they forgot the name of it. They figured that it wouldn't be a problem. It was a Saturday night and they got all dressed up for their big evening in this highly recommended, glamorous celebrity hangout. They got into a taxicab and explained to the driver that they had forgotten the name of this great restaurant but it was one of the best restaurants in town and that it was a man's name. The driver said, "No problem."

They had dinner at Elmer's Pancake House!

Having attained some miniscule celebrity status, I had my ego indulged many times. I started getting personal regards from people who had never spoken to me before—names of relatives I never knew existed. For a while it seemed like I went to school with everybody in New York. Once a woman called me over to her table to show me a charm bracelet with pictures of her grandchildren and on the same bracelet a charm with *my picture on it!* I had even been asked for my autograph on several occasions. But the ultimate ego trip was the following story.

A customer of mine called me from New York and said she just had to tell me what had just happened. She had been shopping and had hailed a taxicab to return to her hotel. On the way, the cab driver inquired where she was from and she said Palm Springs, California. He immediately turned around to her and asked, "Do you know Mel Haber?" (There are probably 40,000 cabs in New York!) When you're big, you're big!

One busy Saturday night, I recognized a face in the crowd that I knew was somebody important. All of a sudden in dawned on me that it was Clive Davis, the head of Arista Records. He was a legend in the music business and I had recently read his biography and recognized him from the pictures in the book. He was standing in the crowded lounge talking with three other men. I went to the Maitre d' and told him to be sure and signal me when he seated Mr. Davis so I could introduce myself.

When the time came for Mr. Davis and his party to be seated, the Maitre d' said, "Mr. Davis, I would like you to meet our owner, Mel Haber." Without even looking at me, Clive Davis handed me his drink and said, "Take this to my table." The Maitre d' looked at me and covered his mouth to hide his laugh. At first I was taken aback as that had never happened before. But, being the consummate restaurateur, I followed them to their table and put the drink down in front of Mr. Davis. As I was walking back to the front of the restaurant, I thought that this was just another funny incident for the book. Just then, I noticed a super public relations agent from Hollywood whom I knew. I walked up to him and laughingly explained what had just happened. He said, "I know Clive Davis very well. Let's go over and tell him the whole story. He will get a kick out of it." We walked back to Mr. Davis' table and the PR agent told Mr. Davis that I was the owner of the restaurant and that when we were introduced, without thinking, he simply put his drink in my hand and told me to carry it to his table. Clive Davis glanced up at me said rather curtly, "Get me another scotch and soda!"

When you're big, you're big!

When You're Welcome, You're Welcome

I was meeting all sorts of important people. John Swearingen, the head of Standard Oil of New Jersey and the head of the Continental Illinois Bank, and his wife, Bonnie, were socially very prominent. Traditionally, during the annual Bob Hope Golf Classic, people who had homes that backed upon the fairways where the tournament was played would hold parties so you could watch the celebrities and pros play while passing behind their homes.

Mr. and Mrs. Swearingen were kind enough to invite my manager and myself to one of these luncheon parties at their home. They told us that President Ford was expected along with Bob Hope and Ginger Rogers. I don't have to tell you how flattered I felt and thought this was a sure sign that I had finally arrived.

While I am not a party-goer by nature, this was one I was certainly not going to miss. As we arrived at the guard gate of the community where they lived, we were cleared immediately as our names were on the guest list. We drove up the street and saw a bunch of cars in front of the home. We pulled in and parked —nervous and excited at the same time. As we entered the home we were warmly greeted by a butler and the living room was quite crowded. There were two different food stations set up in the living room, as well as a bar. We didn't recognize anybody in the room and saw no familiar faces so we each got a drink and tried to look like we belonged.

We searched for our host and hostess but could not find them. We mingled for about 20 minutes, making small talk about the golf tournament with some of the guests. With that, an older woman approached us, introduced herself as Judy's mother and informed us that Judy and Richard would be down in a few minutes. I looked at my manager. My manager looked at me. Judy and Richard?

I timidly went over to the bartender and very quietly asked him the name of the owners of the home only to find out we had walked into the wrong party!

Hello Young Lovers

Astay at Ingleside Inn has been a prize on the television show, *The Dating Game*, for many years. The winners were given a weekend at the Ingleside Inn and were always accompanied by a chaperone. One evening when I arrived to work, the Maitre d' informed me that the winners of *The Dating Game* were seated at a certain table. As I walked by the table it was obvious that they were getting on quite well as they were necking very passionately while the chaperone looked on. When I returned to the Maitre d's stand, I mentioned how well they were getting along and the Maitre d' said, "Mr. Haber, he's necking with the chaperone!"

It Pays To Be Honest

One day I took my car to the car wash. While I was waiting at the other end for my car to come out, a young man, who looked familiar, greeted me and said, "Mr. Haber, how are you?"

Now, during my years in Palm Springs, I had operated five different restaurants in addition to the Ingleside Inn. Because so many people have worked for me in one of the restaurants at one time or another, I assumed that at one time this young man had worked for me. I returned his greeting and, in an attempt to make conversation, I asked him how business was. He said, "We were pretty slow last night." I remarked that we were too and asked him where he worked. He looked at me surprised and, much to my chagrin said, "For you, Mr. Haber!"

Live and Learn

I t was no secret to anybody that I knew very little about the food business. I learned very early that you really can't bluff so I was probably my own best agent in promoting my ignorance.

One evening as I was circulating through the restaurant, a woman called me over and asked, "Melvyn, how is your *Veal Ingleside* prepared?" I responded, "Pardon me, madam. But I know nothing about the food." She looked at me and said, "Melvyn, you told me the same thing ten years ago — you had to learn something in ten years."

I guess I'm not the only one short on knowledge. A regular guest brought in a very special friend of hers who was visiting from New York. At the end of dinner, the gentleman guest asked the waiter if we had any Vandemint (a popular after-dinner cordial). The waiter said, "I'm sorry sir, I don't really know but I will get the captain to help you." The captain appeared and the gentleman repeated the questions as to whether or not we had any Vandemint and the captain quickly responded, "Oh no, he doesn't come in any more."

No Forwarding Address

One of our regular customers owed us approximately $300 when his monthly statement was returned and stamped, Moved With No Forwarding Address. I knew the man and felt sure that he did not mean to stick us for the money but was simply unaware of his debt. Since we could not locate him I simply wrote it off as one of those things.

Several years had passed when one evening my Maitre d' told me that the gentlemen sitting at Table 33 would like to say hello. Lo and behold, it was Mr. Ross, the gentlemen who owed me the money! The fact that he asked to see me only verified that he had no idea that he owed me any money. He was with a female companion and I greeted him like a long lost friend and we chatted for awhile. I didn't want to bring up the money situation in front of the lady, so I told him I would see him before he left. I immediately went over to my manager and told him to make sure he kept an eye on Table 33, that Mr. Ross was sitting there and he owed us money from three years ago. I told him to make sure he got Mr. Ross' new address as he left.

I loved and adored my manager, however, I knew he was not the most alert person in the world. It was a busy Saturday night and just to make sure that he didn't forget about Table 33, I reminded him several times to watch for their departure. Even though I had emphasized how important it was, I still did not feel confident. So I went to the waiter and told him to buy after-dinner drinks for Table 33 and to inform the manager as soon as he did it. I figured that way the manager would be reminded that they were almost ready to leave.

I was talking with some people at the end of the bar when the Maitre d' waved me to the front as Mr. Ross was leaving and wanted to thank me for the after-dinner drinks. I scanned the dining room for the manager but he was nowhere in sight. I couldn't believe it. I ran into the kitchen and sure enough he was standing there talking to the cashier. I virtually screamed at him that Mr. Ross was leaving. He ran out of the kitchen as if he were on fire, almost knocking over several waiters. He ran outside to find Mr. Ross while I returned to the bar.

The next thing I knew an old friend of mine from New York walked into the bar and said, "Melvyn, just because I came in here to say hello to you, why do I have to give your manager my home address?" I had made my manager so nervous he ran up to the wrong man and actually got into an argument with him because my friend wouldn't give him his home address.

That was five years ago and I hope someday Mr. Ross will return.

Potty Prose

A t one time we had two guitar players who strolled and played for the guests in the dining room. They always started in the middle of the evening because we only allowed them to play for the second seating, as we needed the tables turned over from the first seating.

When they first came in for the evening, the guitar players would go downstairs by the men's room and they would store their guitar cases in the wine room which is right opposite the men's room, at the bottom of the steps. They would then stand right outside the men's room warming up their instruments. One night as I was walking around at approximately 8:30 p.m., a couple was walking out the front door. The woman looked down the steps, saw the guitar players rehearsing, and said to her male escort, "Boy, is this place fancy! They have two guitar players in the men's room."

Big Spender

We had this great, black piano player who alternated with a white piano player. We also had a black men's room attendant who worked in a tuxedo and carried two attaché cases to and from work, which held his precious toiletries and whatever other amenities he used to service the customers.

There was a certain 'Big Spender' from the East Coast who had a condominium in Palm Springs, and who frequented Melvyn's bar regularly. One evening about 11 p.m., the 'Big Spender' pulled up in the driveway, and as he was getting out of his car with his lady friend, he saw that the men's room attendant was leaving. The 'Big Spender' assumed he was the piano player and asked him, "Where are you going?" The men's room attendant said, "Home." The 'Big Spender' reached into his pocket, pulled out a ONE HUNDRED DOLLAR BILL, handed it to the guy and said, "Can you hang around another hour?" The bathroom attendant took a look at the $100 bill and said, "YES SIR!" and ran right back into the bathroom, opened his attaché cases and laid out his brushes and toiletries.

Once inside, the 'Big Spender' saw the white piano player and started to look around for the black piano player. He went down to the bathroom, saw the black attendant in the bathroom and said, "What are you doing here?" The bathroom attendant replied, "Well, you asked me to hang around another hour." With that, of course, the guy realized that he had tipped the toilet room attendant by mistake, and came running up to me and said, "You'll never believe what I just did – I tipped the men's room attendant $100..." and told me the story. Thinking it was the funniest thing that had happened in quite a while, I told the story throughout the restaurant immediately. The next day when I got to work, I found that five waiters had put applications on my desk for the job of men's room attendant!

Hollywood's Loss

Cameron Mitchell and Hope Holiday, the famous Hollywood actor and actress became friends of mine through the restaurant, as they were regular customers. One day as they were entertaining some people in Melvyn's, I went over to the table and started chatting. Cameron was ribbing me about all the press I was receiving in the newspapers and magazines as well as appearing on several national TV shows. I commented that with all I had done I had never appeared in a movie. Cameron turned to me, and more to impress his guests than me, said, "You really want to be in a movie? I am filming one now and I've a perfect speaking part for you." I got all excited and said, "Absolutely, I would love to appear in it." He asked me if I had a three-piece white suit, a lot of gold chains, and would they be able to film the scene in a corner of the restaurant. The white suit was no problem; I had bought one my first year in Palm Springs and only worn it once. The gold chains were easy enough to come by from some of the waiters, and the corner of the restaurant as the setting was easy enough to furnish. Cameron told me he was in the middle of filming and producing a movie called *Kill Point* and that it was being shot in the desert, and also had my good friend, Marc Lawrence in it. He said he had a part for me as a South American gun dealer and in the particular scene I would be making a "gun buy." He said it was a speaking part with several lines. I really got excited and asked him when the filming would take place, and he replied in approximately three to four weeks, and he would call me beforehand to set it up.

Approximately three weeks had passed when I got a call from someone who identified himself as Production Assistant for the movie, and that they had scheduled the filming for the following day at 4 o'clock at Melvyn's. The Production Assistant said I should have my gold chains, my three-piece white suit and they would bring in the script AN HOUR EARLIER so I could study my lines. I cannot describe how excited I was.

The next day at approximately 3 p.m., forty people converged on Melvyn's Restaurant...production people, actors, actresses, extras, cameramen and on and on. This really was exciting. The head of production told me that Hope Holiday and Cameron Mitchell were just finishing a scene in Indio and would be along shortly. They gave me a script to study and I was certain I was on the way to stardom. An anxious hour and a half passed with no sign of Cameron and Hope. At approximately 5 p.m., the person in charge of production received a phone call from Cameron, that their car had broken down in Indio, and they would have to reschedule the shooting for a later date. I was informed they would call me 24 hours before the reshooting. Everybody packed up and left. Needless to say, I felt quite disappointed and frustrated.

That was approximately seven years ago and I am still waiting for the call to schedule the shooting. (The movie *Kill Point* was released approximately five years ago!)

Love At First –?

There was a young guy in town who was a frequent customer at the restaurant. He was a regular type guy and often came with various different, but always pretty ladies. One of the more eligible bachelors, so to speak. He was about 37 years old, had been married once, made a reasonably good living, and had no problem enjoying a great social life.

One Saturday night, he was seated in the back of the Lounge with a group of about six people. My girlfriend joined them, and they sat around having drinks and chatting for approximately two hours. I stopped by, chatted for a while, and was introduced to his date. My lady and I left the restaurant about midnight, after we said our good-nights, and went home.

Monday morning this guy called me up, all excited, and told me that after leaving my restaurant that evening, he had flown to Las Vegas and got married. Needless to say, I was very surprised, immediately called my girlfriend and told her that Arnie went and got married to Linda that night. She pointed out immediately that I had made a mistake in names, as the girl he was with was Vickie. It was not uncommon for me to make a mistake in names, so I thought nothing of it. About three or four hours later, Arnie called me back on some other business, and I asked him the name of the girl he married, and he said 'Linda.' Somewhat confused, I told him I had just spoken to my lady who told me he had been with Vickie. He said he was with Vickie, but he married Linda. He went on to explain that about twenty minutes after I left, a young lady came into the restaurant lounge with a guy. He started chatting with her while her date was getting drunk. They went out to the pool and had a drink, and after chatting for another hour they both realized they had found what each was looking for. He suggested they go immediately to Las Vegas to get married, and she agreed. They drove to a small airport in the area to find a plane to Las Vegas, only to find the airport closed and they finally wound up in Los Angeles where they took a regularly scheduled airplane. This really had to be one of the greatest love stories of all times, and as Arnie tells it on the way to the wedding chapel, which incidentally was appropriately named the "We've Only Just Begun Wedding Chapel," Arnie asked his bride-to-be "By the way, what is your last name?"

It wasn't until after they had already been married that Arnold discovered she didn't even live in Palm Springs, but in the Orange County area. At last sighting, they were both deliriously happy, and this story gave me a great inspiration to promote a cocktail party for some locals in town with the invitations reading, "You are invited to a Wedding...maybe even your own!"

Tip–To Insure Promptness

It was a Memorial Day weekend and Melvyn's was jammed. We were really having a great night. A local lady, who was a regular customer, came in and introduced me to the gentleman with her. She asked if we could please squeeze her in and explained that she did not have a reservation as a friend had fixed her up with this man at the last minute. I assured her we would take care of her first. I made sure that she and her date were seated and proceeded to circulate.

I was visiting with some people in the lounge when the woman passed by on the way to the ladies' room and thanked me for taking care of her. No sooner had she walked by than my manager ran up to me and said, "Come quickly! You won't believe what just happened!"

I followed him to the front of the restaurant where a flurry of activity was taking place. I saw all kinds of men leaving through the front door. They were all wearing windbreaker jackets. They read F.B.I. or Sheriff's Department or San Diego Police or Palm Springs Police. It seems that the lady's date was a big time swindler and every law enforcement agency was after him. I followed the men outside and saw that they even had a helicopter hovering overhead.

Evidently they had waited until the lady left the table and then swooped in with guns drawn, handcuffed him and whisked him out of the restaurant. The entire episode took only a few minutes. One of the officers informed us that he was wanted in several counties for fraud. The manager jokingly said, "At least you could have waited until he paid the check!" Out of curiosity, the officer asked how much it was and the manager told him that he had ordered an expensive bottle of wine with the meal and his check was $140. Needless to say, the incident was the talk of the restaurant in spite of the fact that it happened so quickly that half of the patrons never even knew what happened.

When the lady returned to the table she resumed eating her salad assuming her date must have gone to the men's room. After waiting about 20 minutes for him to return she asked me to check the men's room to see if he was O.K. When I told her what happened her comment was, "I just knew he was too good to be true!"

About two hours later I was chatting with my Maitre d' about the evening's events when one of our local police officers came in and handed me $140 that he had taken out of the swindler's pocket to pay the restaurant bill. I was overwhelmed and was trying to think how to thank him when the Maitre d' said, "Hey, what about the tip?"

P.S. The swindler's bail was set at nine million dollars! It turned out that he was on the San Diego Police Department's Ten Most Wanted List!

Some Boosts to the Ego
for the Owner of a Place
Catering to "The Rich and Famous"

When making arrangements with Mr. Sinatra for his pre-wedding dinner, I remarked, "What a great honor to have your party at Melvyn's." Whereupon Mr. Sinatra said, "C'mon kid, your mesh-bugah!" (The Jewish word for family.)

Carol Burnett proudly giving her family a tour of the grounds of the Ingleside Inn as if it were her own home.

After spending three nights hanging out with me at my various restaurants, Richard Pryor invited me to accompany him to the Academy Awards.

Following being married at the Ingleside Inn, June Allyson sent me a huge blown-up picture of her wedding party with the following inscription on it, "Everybody should be married at the Ingleside Inn at least once in their lifetime."

A customer of Melvyn's restaurant had just returned from a celebrity golf tournament in Las Vegas and said that when he told his celebrity partner that he was from Palm Springs, Joe DiMaggio replied, "I have a good friend there, do you know Mel Haber?" (Mr. DiMaggio had stayed at the Inn the previous week and I was thrilled and honored to have met him for the first time.)

Goldie Hawn and Kurt Russell flew down in his new private plane just to have lunch poolside at the Ingleside Inn. They took a quick swim after lunch and then flew back to Los Angeles.

When Rita Hayworth came out of the hospital she insisted on recuperating at only one place… The Ingleside Inn.

I had the pleasure of meeting and dancing with Joan Collins at my nightclub, Cecil's. The next day I found her photograph personally autographed with a lovely thank you note on my desk.

Michelle Phillips drove up from Mexico just to celebrate her 50th birthday at the Ingleside Inn and Melvyn's Restaurant. Debbie Reynolds celebrated her 50th at Melvyn's as well. (So did Melvyn Haber.)

When the famous author, David Heyman, came in to Melvyn's, I immediately handed him a copy of his latest book *Liz* to autograph for my collection. He wrote, "And I enjoyed reading your book as well." (It turned out that he had stayed at the Ingleside Inn several months before and had enjoyed reading my *Bedtime Stories!*)

IN CLOSING

I have made many unsuccessful attempts over the years to put this book together. What started out as simply telling a few interesting stories turned into a test of my memory and writing ability. I am not sure which is worse.

There seems to be an endless list of amusing incidents and characters that I have encountered over what is now a twenty year career of owning and operating five different restaurants and an elegant Inn in the land of the "Rich and Famous." Some of the truly great stories will have to wait until the people are no longer living or until I can't remember if they are or not.

I hope you enjoyed reading about these experiences as I certainly enjoyed living them. To be continued and thank you!

— Melvyn "Hemingway" Haber